WILD WINGS
TO THE NORTHLANDS

Wild Wings
to the
Northlands

A Bird-watcher's Spring Journey
from the Mediterranean
to the Arctic Sea

S. BAYLISS SMITH

H. F. & G. WITHERBY LTD.
61-62 Watling Street, London, E.C.4

SBN 85493 071 X

Printed in Great Britain by
Ebenezer Baylis and Son Limited
The Trinity Press, Worcester, and London

Foreword

by GUY MOUNTFORT

President of the British Ornithologists' Union

THE pioneers of ornithology carried shotguns. Though they often sentimentalized about the beauties of the birds they shot, their chief satisfaction came from their cabinets of neatly labelled skins. Nevertheless, their contribution to our knowledge of species and distribution was valuable, much as we may deplore the excesses to which the passion for collecting was often carried.

Today's ornithologist, like the author of this book, studies the bird as a living creature. Armed with binoculars, a camera and a tape-recorder, he knows far more about his subject than his forebears would have imagined to be possible. The new science of ethology — the study of behaviour — has far outstripped the interests of the shotgun school. Birds and other animals are now intensively studied on an organized international basis and in most countries at least the rarer species are today protected by law. Man is beginning to recognize that they are not only a source of constant enjoyment, but an irreplaceable part of his natural heritage, which he must safeguard.

The amateur bird-watcher provides the bulk of interest on which modern ornithology now flourishes.

The many local and national ornithological societies in
Great Britain are largely dependent on him for their
organized investigations and he readily conforms to the
high scientific standard demanded for such work.
Thanks largely to his interest we now have a network
of well-managed bird sanctuaries, which enable everyone to see the majority of the British species thriving in
secure protection. The steady flow of accurate information obtained from amateur bird-watchers on their
travels has made the British Isles ornithologically the
best documented area in the world.

In western Europe a similar growth of interest in
wild birds and their protection has been growing
steadily in recent years. In Holland and the Scandinavian
countries it is widespread and of long standing. Even in
the Latin countries it is growing, only Italy still
legalizing the massive slaughter of migratory song-
birds which used to occur elsewhere. Thanks to the
efforts of the World Wildlife Fund, Spain can now
boast of its magnificent and well guarded Coto Doñana
National Park and even Italy has its Abruzzi and other
reserves. Probably the best known of all the continental
sanctuaries is, of course, France's superb Camargue,
which is where this book begins. It is now one of the
chief centres of ornithological research and very different
from the wild region which I first visited forty years
ago.

To the many thousands of people who now go bird-
watching in Europe, *Wild Wings to the Northlands* will
be invaluable. It is a stimulating *vade mecum* to anyone
wishing to visit the most rewarding reserves, though I
suspect that few will have the stamina to complete Stan

6

Bayliss Smith's strenuous itinerary on a single occasion. Old hands at the game, who have faced the mistral to watch Flamingoes behind Sainte Marie de la Mer, or who have trudged the quaking bogs of Lapland under a sky full of the music of Golden Plovers, will find nostalgic enjoyment in every page.

Stan Bayliss Smith writes with infectious enthusiasm and admirably describes the thrills of discovering longed-for treasures in far-away places. His comments are nonetheless made with the careful accuracy of a practised observer. Though primarily interested in birds, he gives a well-balanced portrayal of the varied scenes through which he passes, from the Mediterranean to the Arctic Sea. In short, this is a book which should appeal to everyone who enjoys exploration and the beauties of nature.

Contents

Illustrations

ILLUSTRATIONS

I

The Open Door

FROM the Mediterranean to the Arctic Sea is a distance
of well over two thousand miles. For countless birds
this is the last lap of a migratory journey that started
thousands of miles further south, and yet, every spring,
with unfailing regularity, they make this arduous journey to the northlands, impelled by the urge to rear their
families in the Land of the Midnight Sun.

What pleasures might lie in store for a bird-watching
enthusiast if he could follow the same route, starting in
the Camargue in mid-April, and arriving in northern
Lapland by the middle of June in time to experience the
splendour of an Arctic spring? To be truly worthwhile
the journey ought not to be a haphazard affair. It should
be carefully planned to enable visits to be paid to the
many bird sanctuaries and nature reserves that would lie
along the route.

To undertake such a journey was an ambition that my
brother and I had shared for many years. But, like many
ambitions, it seemed very far from fulfilment, chiefly
because, although my brother could conceivably extract
himself from business commitments at this time of year,
I was not in a position to do likewise. A headmaster
cannot disappear from his school for two-thirds of the

summer term without very good reason. To ask for compassionate leave to go gallivanting across Europe on a glorified birds-nesting foray was simply not on. No governing body could be expected to treat it as a serious proposal. And so summer term succeeded summer term, and 'North with the Spring' was relegated to the realm of wishful thinking. And there it would have stayed, but for my brother's tenacity of purpose and the very generous attitude adopted by the governing body of my school.

Since our boyhood spent in the Derbyshire hills, my brother and I had been under the spell of wildlife and wild places, with birds a particular concern, and the family of waders a special interest. Some of our happiest adventures had taken place at a later date when, living nearer the coast, we had spent long hours in concealment on mud-flats and salt marshes in pursuit of these elusive creatures. Photographically we were 'tide-liners', confining our activities mainly to the seasons of wader passage, when these globe-spanners were hastening to and from their breeding-grounds in the far north.

But should we ever have the opportunity of visiting the northlands where they nested – those vast marsh areas of Lapland, or the limitless tundras fronting the Arctic Sea? Could we ever contrive to be there during the few brief weeks in which the ceremonies of courtship are observed, the eggs laid, and the young ones reared in the arctic solitudes?

It was my brother who really precipitated events by threatening that, come what might, he proposed making an expedition to Lapland in fifteen months time – and what about it? My only hope lay in the fact that in exalted academic spheres sabbatical leave was sometimes granted to members of the profession with a record of long service behind them. I was, in fact, approaching the completion of twenty years of headmastership. Perhaps a hint could be given in the right quarter. Discreetly the hint was given – but what would be the outcome? There followed weeks of almost unbearable suspense. The matter was, no doubt, under consideration, but no word came. At last I could bear the suspense no longer, and I wrote to the Chairman to ask if a decision had been taken. The Chairman, a member of Her Majesty's Judiciary, was not given to wasting time or words. His reply, laconic but decisive, came on a postcard. 'You are pushing an open door!' It later transpired that the Council had given my suggestion their sympathetic approval at a meeting held three months prior to my impetuous letter. There had, however, been a slight misunderstanding as to who should convey the good news to me, with the result that it was not conveyed at all. Feeling more than a little bewildered, I hastened to convey my thanks. At last it had come – the long-awaited chance of a lifetime! In twelve months' time I should be experiencing an Arctic spring. For the rest of the summer term I was walking on air.

But now came the hard planning, not only of the expedition itself, but of the cover for my period of absence from school. From my Second Master and from my colleagues on the staff came a magnificent response. I need have no fears about the welfare of the school in my absence. From my brother came a shout of delighted approval at the prospect of a joint expedition, and also a generous assurance on his part that all the transport arrangements, both practical and financial, would be his responsibility.

We met at the end of term and had long discussions on the route that we should take and on what we should attempt to do, and the expedition gradually took shape. It was to be a journey with an underlying purpose. We shared a common concern for wildlife and its conservation. Could we not, on this journey, find out what conservation projects were being undertaken in the countries through which we should pass? There must surely be like-minded people who would help us. The establishing of primary contacts was a first essential, and here, Ian Macphail who was then Director-General of the World Wildlife Fund in Britain, Sir Hugh Elliott of the Nature Conservancy, Peter Conder of the R.S.P.B., and Stanley Cramp of *British Birds* were able to make most valuable suggestions and to put us in touch with conservation authorities abroad.

A photographic record of the journey was envisaged, and possibly tape-recordings of bird-song encountered en route. At first there was no suggestion of venturing into the realm of film-making, but John King, a loyal friend and ally, and secretary of the local W.W.F. Committee, on hearing of the proposed journey, lured me into attempting a film record with the loan of a magnificent Paillard-Bolex 16 mm. ciné camera with its battery of lenses. The weight and bulk of our combined apparatus, when finally assembled, was enough to make the stoutest heart quail. Our only hope lay in the efficiency of our transport. The journey up to Lapland should present no problems. Our sturdy Bedford with Sprite caravan in tow would provide us with almost luxurious travelling accommodation. But what of the far north? We envisaged a stage at which we might have to leave the caravan behind and press on with the Bedford un-encumbered. We even considered the possibility of being forced eventually to abandon the Bedford and don ruck-sacks in our final bid for the Arctic Sea. It all sounded very romantic and decidedly hazardous. In fact, when we reached the far north we found that we could, with caution and a fair amount of rattling and bumping along the gravel roads, keep pressing on with the caravan still more or less in one piece, and, to our great satisfaction, not only reach the Arctic Sea at Porsanger Fjord, but continue eastwards for another hundred and fifty miles until we finally came to rest by the side of a little bay, where we looked across the opalescent waters of Varanger Fjord at the grim, snow-streaked mountains of arctic Russia.

We visualized a journey down to the Mediterranean, up to the Arctic Sea and back to Britain, of perhaps six thousand miles, but that did not take into account the almost daily excursions into inviting country along side roads and cart tracks that promised adventure and good bird-watching all along the route. In the end we found that we had persuaded the Bedford to nose its way along nine thousand miles of roadways of one sort and another – good, bad, and execrable – in the course of its three months of gruelling travel. To its eternal credit it main-tained an even temper and an even temperature throughout – except once, when, failing a supply of one of the customary brands, it was temporarily filled up with a local Lap brew, concocted, we suspect, of wood alcohol and paraffin, when it grew a little hot under the collar and registered its protest accordingly. A dash of 100 per cent octane at the next filling station quickly restored its equanimity.

The Sprite caravan stood up to its shattering experience magnificently. It was bumped and bounced over two thousand miles of pot-holed and corrugated roads in the far north and still survived. It sustained a black eye in the process: we lost a window when a passing lorry showered us with flying stones. It sheared a bolt from its under-carriage when, near Karigasniemi, we hit a huge pot-hole in the road – a cavity deep enough, we considered, to have provided decent burial for one of the reindeer that frequently crossed the road ahead of us in those northern parts. By the greatest good fortune, however, we carried a spare bolt. After an hour's strenuous 'jacking-up', in the course of which we assembled sufficient boulders to erect, on completion of the job, a commemorative cairn by the roadside, we put matters right and resumed our northern progress.

One impression of the journey will always remain with us – the friendliness and helpfulness of all whom we encountered on our way. Our linguistic ability was minimal, but it never seemed seriously to matter. In the most unlikely places we usually found someone with a smattering of English who was only too pleased to engage in conversation with us. I recollect particularly two fifteen-year-old Swedish boys, out for an evening ride on their motor-scooters, who stopped to talk to us. We had drawn up on the roadside in northern Sweden at the head of the Bothnian Gulf. With a charming blend of diffidence and eagerness they approached us. It transpired that they had never talked to Englishmen before, and

16

they wanted to try out the conversational phrases that they had learnt in the classroom of the local village school. How many English boys of their age, I wondered, would have taken advantage of an opportunity to talk in a foreign language to strangers passing through their country?

Another lasting impression was the close bond that exists between fellow members of the Confraternity of Caravanners on the highways of Europe – always the cheery wave of the hand or the quick recognition flash of headlights as one passed a fellow caravanner on the road. And often, too, when we had stopped for a brief inspection of the brakes or the towing-gear, a fellow-traveller would stop to inquire if we were in difficulties or needed help in any way. It was a pleasant surprise to find, particularly in the Scandinavian countries, that road-builders have recognized that travellers require to stop from time to time by the roadside for rest and refreshment and for other elementary needs. How welcome it was to be able to draw off the road at a resting place, screened with shrubs and trees, with tables and benches provided for a picnic meal, with proper facilities for the disposal of litter – and, quite often, with simple but entirely adequate toilet facilities. Perhaps the greatest surprise of this kind was to discover, at Adamsfjord, away up on the Arctic Sea coast, near to a splendid waterfall that would tempt most travellers to halt for a few minutes, two charming little cabins, gaily painted in red and green and scarcely recognizable at first for the purpose that they were there to serve: and on their doorways, neatly and discreetly inscribed, the simple words 'Adam' and 'Eva'.

2

2

South to the Mediterranean

IT WAS April 11th on a flawless spring morning that we set forth from Newhaven on the cross-Channel Ferry. No expedition could have had a more auspicious start. The day was windless and the Channel a mill-pond.

For the opening stages of our adventure there were to be six in the party, but at the end of April we should be saying farewell to our wives, and to my two young daughters who would be returning to school for the summer term.

For the month of May my brother and I would be exploring nature reserves in Belgium, Holland and Denmark on our own. For the final month in Lapland my younger son, Tim, who had just left school and was waiting to go off on Voluntary Service Overseas for a year, would be joining us. It seemed a good idea for him to have the opportunity of crossing the Arctic Circle before being dispatched to the British Solomon Islands away out in the Coral Sea.

We had the smoothest of crossings to Dieppe, and even the Herring Gulls, usually faithful attendants on these occasions, decided that there were more jolly things to do on an exhilarating spring morning than to stay hanging about the stern of a cross-Channel boat, on the off-chance of a pail of kitchen waste being tipped overboard. We soon left the gulls behind, and it was only as we neared the French coast that we made our first bird observation. A few miles offshore we butted our way through a small raft of Guillemots. There was a sudden spatter on either side of the boat: the glassy surface of the Channel was momentarily ruffled by stampeding wings and feet, but the Guillemots did not fly far, and, recovering their composure, watched us at a safe distance as we trundled on our way.

We passed through the customs at Dieppe with a minimum of formality, and were soon humming along the road to Paris through a countryside very like the Sussex we had left behind, except for the absence of hedgerows and the steady increase of mistletoe on orchard trees. Roadside poplars began to appear, and telephone wires were festooned with fallen catkins that leaned into the breeze and looked for all the world like miniature Swallows clinging there. Cherry orchards were in bridal array. Windflowers were nodding by the roadsides. Meadows were gay with dandelions, and, as a reminder that it was Palm Sunday and a festival, village children were carrying nosegays of cowslips gathered from the fields. Following the course of the lovely, tree-fringed, green-islanded Seine we already had the feeling that we were visibly overtaking spring as we journeyed along. As we neared our destination at Versailles we passed through orchards of blossoming pears, and arrived in the evening at our caravan site where hazels and beech trees were in tender leaf, horn-beams adorned with the palest of green flowers, and a

Redstart singing bravely from the leafy canopy just above our caravan roof. But, alas, for fickle April weather. A blustery wind arose during the night, and a heavy rain shower at dawn gave us a foretaste of the weather in store for us during our day of sight-seeing in Paris and Versailles.

We were on the road and heading south by half-past eight the following morning, speeding through the forest of Fontainebleau with its strange, heavily bouldered woodland. A Carrion Crow, pecking at a flattened rabbit corpse on the highway, barely stepped aside as we hustled past. A few miles on and we disturbed a pair of Magpies engaged in the same macabre search for protein. Fontainebleau called for a short halt, and gave us the opportunity to make some purchases in the open market there. We noted a high-enclosing wall which told of a bird sanctuary within, but the south was calling and we did not pause to investigate. On, relentlessly on, we sped. Townships flashed past. Endless advertisements bombarded us. At first the advertisements amused, but after a time they grew wearisome. But we never tired of the roadside trees, trimmed and naked up to their shoulders, and all through central France they were festooned with mistletoe – great, dark green clusters standing out clear against the blue sky. Near Avallon we halted for a while to enjoy the sight of meadows, lavender-hued with cuckoo flowers, flanked with hedgerows frothy with blackthorn blossom. After Avallon we entered Charolais country where fields were dotted with splendid white cattle of this distinctive breed. Then up we soared over high hills of pale buff rock, and so, down to Chalon-sur-Saône, its terraced vineyards glowing in the evening sun, to a camp and caravan site near the river, with meadow grass drenched with dew, and a full-throated chorus of frogs as a background to our preparations for the night.

Before leaving the following morning we spent some time watching the frog-catchers at work. They were collecting the night's catch, working along their lines of floating tins strung out across the shallow pools by the river side. A few early Swallows were hawking for insects over the water. The quest for protein takes many forms.

Southwards we went, down the E.7 with its endless stream of hooting cars and lorries. The barrage of advertisements continued, but it was now the inconspicuous and homely signs that entertained us. 'Chien méchant' on a farm gate, and 'Dormez au calme!' on a roadside hotel. Some hope, on the E.7! We gratefully left the main road at Mâcon, and made a detour to the east that would take in a low-lying area near Villars les Dombes. M. de Vilmorin, Director-General of the 'Société Nationale de Protection de la Nature', had suggested that we might pay a visit to a newly-created reserve on the outskirts of the town. A score of Black-headed Gulls feeding by an open drain near Bourg proclaimed the near presence of marshland, and, just outside Villars les Dombes we passed two reedy meres where we had our first distant views of Black-winged Stilts feeding with Godwits in the shallows there.

We presented our credentials at the Town Hall, and had a cordial exchange of greetings with three dignitaries there. We were given a large photostat copy of a map of the reserve, and were escorted thither and then left to our own devices and told that we could go where we liked and explore to our heart's content. This new reserve is in a 'wetland' area of partially flooded meadow land. It is intersected by the Bourg–Lyons road, and is bounded on its western side by a railway embankment. It was clear that, with a minimum of expense in the way of upkeep, it could provide a valuable refuge for migrating ducks and waders in a popular wild-fowling area. A Marsh Harrier was quartering the reed beds. Pochards and Mallard were feeding on an open stretch of water. Spotted Redshanks, Godwits and many small waders were working along the muddy edges of the pools. Lapwings were nesting in the open grassland, and a Coot had a full clutch of eggs in her nest in a clump of sedge. It was a pleasant watery oasis of marsh and meadow in which to spend an hour or two on an April afternoon. We went on our way refreshed, and confirmed in the belief that more refuges of this kind are urgently needed. The 'Wetlands Survey' carried out in recent years by the I.U.C.N. indicates that the thoughts of conservationists are more and more turning in this direction. A chain of refuges sited along migration routes could make all the difference between survival and otherwise for a great many birds that must use a watery site such as this when passing to and from their northern breeding grounds and their winter quarters.

Between Villars les Dombes and Lyons we passed over high ground again, and had distant views of the snow-covered Alps before dropping down to the valley of the Rhône. Lyons, with its tall blocks of flats in geometrical silhouette against the skyline, we by-passed successfully, and then, suddenly, just before Tain, the steeply-terraced vineyards of L'Hermitage, splendidly shadowed in the evening sun, came into view. We drew off the road on to a stretch of greensward beside the broad and swiftly-flowing Rhône. Flying up river at steady intervals Marsh Harriers came winnowing past. They had the purposeful look of birds on migration. They were coming up from the south, from the Rhône delta. They made the Camargue seem very near. Tomorrow, by this time, we should be there.

The following morning, the air warm and still, we sped south down the Rhône valley into the heart of spring. White lilac was in fragrant bloom, and cottage porches were hung with festoons of lavender-hued wistaria. Vines were sprouting in the vineyards that lined our route, and fresh green leaves were showing. Plane trees had now replaced poplars on the roadsides, and the further south we went the more they leaned in that direction, mute evidence of the effect of countless years of relentless pressure from the dreaded Mistral – that searing blast of chilling air that funnels down the Rhône valley, often for weeks on end, as an icy air stream from the north moves down to take the place of warm air rising from the Mediterranean Sea. On all sides there were signs of how an agricultural landscape is conditioned by its prevailing wind. Farmhouses huddled behind conifer plantations and high bamboo windbreaks. On a mild and windless April morning it was difficult to appreciate the necessity for such protective measures. A few days later we were to discover for ourselves the acute discomforts of Mistral conditions, but for the present, with the air balmy and still, the Provençal countryside was very lovely and inviting.

At Orange we rested for an hour. We examined the Roman triumphal arch, still in a remarkable state of preservation. Nowhere in France does the measured tread of the Roman legions sound closer.

A cheerful snatch of canary-like song from a near-by plane tree disclosed to us a new bird for our check-list – the Serin Finch, and a walk through the tree-lined market square produced for us a puzzling feature of continental bird song that was to re-occur on more than one occasion. A bird was singing in the tree canopy, and the snatch of song with its see-saw repetitions was reminiscent of a Great Tit in an English garden, but the pitch was different and the intonation most peculiar. The binoculars eventually established the identity of the songster beyond all question. It was a Great Tit – continental race: in fact, a Great Tit with a French accent. The positive identification was not, however, satisfactorily made before a great many honest citizens of Orange, observing two Englishmen gazing upwards at a seemingly invisible object in the tree-tops in the crowded market square, were confirmed in their belief that we are, as a race, inclined to eccentricity.

And now we went on, through arid, 'maquis' country towards Avignon, past hillsides littered with massive, rounded boulders, water-rolled for incredible distances through epochs of snow-melt and flood. On through the red-soiled vineyards of Château Neuf du Pape, and so to Avignon, with a view from the Palais des Papes of the celebrated 'Pont', and of the sun-bleached, rosy-tiled

roofs of Provence. It was a countryside soaked in sunshine. It breathed Cézanne and Van Gogh.

On again, through Tarascon and its rich farmlands
levelling out as we approached the delta land: vineyards
and rice fields often enough in adjacent plots. Some of
the rice fields were already partially flooded and tillage
was proceeding. Thus we arrived in the late afternoon
at Arles, aware of a green flush spreading over the whole
of the Mediterranean hinterland. For the first time since
leaving England we could leave the caravan windows
wide open. A cockchafer came buzzing into the lighted
interior in the warm dusk. Nous sommes arrivés!

One important task, however, still had to be performed before nightfall. To visit the reserve area of the
Camargue it was necessary to obtain an official permit
from M. Tallon who resided in the town of Arles.
Armed with correspondence previously conducted with
Dr. Luc Hoffman, Director of the Camargue Biological
Station, we arrived at M. Tallon's residence and were
ushered into his presence. An illustrious and venerable
naturalist of the Camargue, M. Tallon received us with
great courtesy. He was tall, and patriarchal in appearance, with a handsome white beard and a high-domed
forehead. We conversed with him through the medium
of his charming secretary who had that necessary and
fluent command of both languages that neither of us
possessed. I have no clear recollection of the wealth of
fascinating natural history material with which his study
was crowded, but one memory remains. Close by his
elbow, and apparently scrutinizing his signature on
permits to visit the reserve, stood a tall, rose-pink and
white Flamingo, a magnificent specimen and so life-like

that its stillness alone compelled one to conclude that it was not a living bird but a masterpiece of the taxidermist's art. For a naturalist who had spent his whole life in the cause of conservation in the Camargue it was a fitting symbol.

3

April in the Camargue

I<small>T WAS</small> in brilliant sunshine that we set forth the following morning for our first visit to 'La Réserve Zoologique et Biologique du Camargue'. As we left Arles a magnificent Swallowtail butterfly flitted across the road just ahead of us – an auspicious start for the day. For several miles we traversed an area of dyke-intersected fields reminiscent of the Lincolnshire fenlands. Evidence of the increasing importance of rice-growing in this area was plain to see. Until 1939 Spain and Italy were the only rice-growing countries in Europe. Today, paddy-fields cover a quarter of the entire Camargue delta, and their produce now makes France self-sufficient in this cereal. But there are subtle changes in environment taking place as a result of rice-growing. So greedy is rice for sweet water, that in the course of a year enough water is drawn off from the Rhône to cover the delta with a three-foot-deep lake. A lot of this water drains off into the marshes, and some of it penetrates down to subterranean deposits of salt which dissolve and rise to the surface. Thus the degree of brackishness in the marsh water is constantly changing, and this affects the lives of fish and many other living creatures. The subject is one of many that

27

are being studied at the Biological Station in the heart of the reserve.

We were making for the Étang de Vaccares, a vast shallow lake that forms the core of the reserve, and our first sight of the étang was an impressive one. A gap in the tall reeds fringing the shore suddenly disclosed a lake of gloriously clear blue water extending as far as the eye could see. Swimming close to the margin were two Red-crested Pochards, and quartering the reed beds a short distance away were no less than four Marsh Harriers. In the next mile or two we halted a dozen times to watch Purple Herons flying past, to admire the impeccable snowy plumage of Little Egrets delicately picking their way through the marsh grass, to identify a grey-blue Montagu's Harrier rising from a patch of reeds, to gaze enchanted at a pair of Hoopoes swooping low across the road just ahead of us. Penduline Tits were sighted in a clump of tamarisk, and from the obscurity of the dense reed jungle came the occasional 'wumph' of a booming Bittern. And all the time, overhead, a steady stream of hirundine migration was taking place. Flying low, a huge, scythe-winged Swift with a gleaming white belly sped past – it was our first Alpine Swift.

We passed La Capellière, the first 'gardien's' cottage, where Penduline Tits were again lurking in the tamarisks, and were soon at Salin du Badin where we saw an emerald green tree frog clinging to a bamboo by the roadside. Then back again to a turn in the road that led down to Tour de Valat and the Biological Station. But it took us a long time to cover the next half-mile, for twenty-five Black-winged Stilts were feeding daintily in the shallow marsh by the side of the road. They were in the lee of an island of tamarisks that gave them partial shelter from the wind that was now freshening – tall, spider-legged waders with dazzling black and white plumage: curious, exotic birds that looked as though they might well have strayed here out of some Chinese tapestry.

We were not able to make immediate contact with Dr. Hoffman or his assistant, Alan Johnston, as they were both out in the reserve, but we met several of the students and learnt from them that Bee-eaters had not yet arrived but were expected daily, and that Little Egrets and Night Herons were still using a roost in a nearby wood, and we could see them in the late afternoon if we cared to return. As we left the Biological Station a Wryneck flew across the road and alighted, woodpecker fashion, on a tree a few yards away, giving us a quick but satisfactory view of a bird that is now very scarce indeed in England. Following the rough salt-works road to the coast, we trundled along towards Les Saintes Maries. Black-headed Gulls were brawling in the ditches. Several obscure warblers were briefly glimpsed flitting low from bush to bush. A desultory passage of waders was taking place. A party of Greenshanks flew over with clear, ringing 'tew-tew-tew' cries, and a few Terns were also sighted – one of which was probably a 'Gull-bill' but we could not be certain.

As we approached Les Saintes Maries the marshland birds thinned out. The fields were now taken over by white Camargue horses, and by herds of black bulls, peaceful enough when browsing, but pawing the dust menacingly when approached. We always took the precaution of having a wide ditch between us and the bulls. Bull-baiting is a traditional sport in the Roman amphitheatres hereabouts. If you are wise you give these fierce, black bulls a very wide berth.

As a Mediterranean holiday resort Les Saintes Maries was disappointing. It was thronged with holiday crowds and noisy with portable transistors. On the outskirts of the town some interesting equestrian activity was taking place, but we did not stay long, and gratefully returned to our quiet, tree-fringed caravan site at Arles in the late afternoon.

The following morning we set off for a second visit to the reserve, approaching this time by a road that skirted the northern edge of the étang. We halted the Bedford close to a promising stretch of flat marshland. Quail were calling in a near-by field of lucerne, and Crested Larks were trotting along the roadside. But the birds we were hoping to see should be on the distant, mud-caked edges of a swampy region that stretched for half a mile beside the road at this point. Other bird-watchers were already lining the roadside with binoculars at the ready. Some had telescopes trained on the distant mud. We joined a Bavarian schoolmaster and his family, and soon discovered that we were both there for the same purpose – to see our first Pratincoles. Nor were we disappointed. Out there on the caked mud were half a dozen curiously elongated, plover-like birds with light buff throats. After a while two of them took flight, and then it was that the bird-book description of 'huge brown, Swallow-like birds with deeply-forked, black and white tails' exactly fitted. It was a positive identification and a highly satisfactory one. We said goodbye to the friendly Bavarian family and returned to the car. A few minutes later another naturalist – an enthusiast from Switzerland – stopped to ask us if we had seen the Pratincoles. They were not here yesterday, he said. They must have arrived overnight – just in time for the invasion of Easter bird-watchers.

Shortly afterwards, near the 'gardien's' house at Salin du Badin, a young French ornithologist from Marseilles, observing the binoculars slung round our necks, came up to inquire what we had seen that morning, and, in return for news of the Pratincoles, insisted on showing us his own private discovery – a Mallard's nest with eggs by the edge of a ditch a few yards from the road. We all had to take photographs of the nest, the French boy insisting with Gallic courtesy and a twinkle in his eye that the Englishmen 'shoot' first. 'We have a saying from the wars of olden times: "Let the English shoot first," ' he said. 'Do you have a saying like that?' 'Wait till you see the whites of their eyes,' we told him. 'That's good. That's very good,' he said. 'I will remember that.' We shook hands and said goodbye. 'Au revoir – Good Shooting!' he called out as he hopped into his little sports car. We had many pleasant encounters with fellow naturalists during our brief stay in the Camargue, but I particularly remember the quarter of an hour that we spent in the company of that gay, enthusiastic French youth. The setting was so essentially 'Camargue' – the wide blue sky, and the shimmer of sun on the waters of the lovely étang: the squealing of Water Rails in the reed beds near at hand: the croaking of frogs, and the conversational 'tsi-tsi-tsi' of Penduline Tits in the tamarisks: and a glorious

Camberwell Beauty butterfly – the first that I had ever seen alive – gaily flitting past as we stood there talking by the roadside.

After lunch we decided to make for the saline marsh again, along the rough road to the salt works. We were soon halted by the sight of a traffic casualty – a yard-long snake threshing out its life in the dust by the roadside. A passing car had broken its back. As we knelt over it, the Swiss naturalist whom we had met earlier at the Pratincole area came hurrying up. He immediately identified it as a Montpelier snake, promptly dived into the back of his car, and produced a polythene bag from which he extracted an exceedingly lively specimen of the same breed. He was, it seemed, both ornithologist and herpetologist, and was collecting living specimens to take back to his students in Switzerland.

After this informative interlude we continued on our way, and, on the salt flats to the east of the Étang de Vaccares we counted ninety Ruffs and Reeves that had not been there the previous day. A strong wader passage was taking place and birds were continually flying over. But light was beginning to fail and we had a rendezvous with Little Egrets that should soon be flocking to their roost in the trees not far from the Biological Station. By the time we reached the roost the trees were already thronged with birds. We refrained from approaching too close for fear of disturbing them, but it was still light enough for us to count upwards of a hundred Little Egrets clustering thickly on the branches. There were Night Herons and Purple Herons there, too, and a host of noisy Jackdaws. It was a fitting end to another memorable day.

The following morning – Easter Sunday – we went to the ancient cathedral church of St. Trophime in Arles, and afterwards watched some gay and colourful folk-dancing in the cathedral square. The town was in festive mood, and the crowds had assembled not only to watch the dancing but also to witness the traditional parade of Camargue horses and their riders through the town. In the afternoon we visited Les Baux, a ruined medieval stronghold in the high limestone escarpment to the north-east of Arles, and, from the battlements, we saw a solitary Alpine Swift hurtling past in the clear, cold mountain air. On the return journey we stopped for a brief exploration of a stretch of upland scrub, and saw our first Subalpine Warblers – elusive creatures that kept well under cover and scuttered off at our approach with 'tick.tick.tick' notes reminiscent of a Whitethroat.

I was up early the following morning before the others were stirring, and went for a solitary stroll along country lanes on the outskirts of the town. Birds were not plentiful. Most of the species that one would have seen in a similar setting in England were strangely absent – no Blackbirds or Thrushes, no Starlings or Robins, no Rooks or Woodpigeons. There were plenty of House Sparrows, and a few Greenfinches and Gold-finches. A Great Tit was singing with that peculiar intonation that we had heard at Orange. A solitary Garden Warbler gave a brief outburst of song as I passed a wayside copse, but, all in all, it was a singularly unprofitable walk.

And then, as I was nearing the caravan and reflecting on the paucity of bird life in the environs of Arles, there came from the sky above a succession of high-pitched fluty calls that immediately transported me back to a sandpit in Sussex in the summer of 1955, when, for the first time in the annals of British ornithology, Bee-eaters successfully reared their young in Britain. There, flying purposefully overhead in a north-easterly direction, and calling as he flew, was a splendid Bee-eater. I watched him out of sight and returned, jubilant, for breakfast.

With the promise of another fine day we decided to revisit the Étang de Vaccares, if only to satisfy the desire of every bird enthusiast visiting the region to have a glimpse – even though a distant one – of Camargue Flamingoes. The western side of the étang seemed the most likely area in which they might be seen.

The winter population of Flamingoes in the Camargue is usually between one and two thousand birds, but the temporary springtime population may rise to as many as twenty thousand. But during recent years the Camargue Flamingoes have been facing a domestic crisis. An island within the lagoon on which they had made their mud-pie nests for many years became, as a result of their occupation, denuded of its vegetation. Continual wave action eventually wore the island away until it virtually disappeared. The Flamingoes were then compelled to transfer their nesting operations to the edge of the marshland. Here predators of various kinds, foxes and wild boars in particular, wrought havoc amongst eggs and young. From a hatching of 2,200 chicks in 1957 the number had fallen by 1960 to 1,600. In 1961 only 240 chicks survived, and since then very few young have been successfully reared. Meanwhile the original island has been reconstituted, but the

Flamingoes have only recently begun to overcome their suspicion of a man-made island. There is therefore a deep concern for the future of the Camargue Flamingoes for no species can survive without the means of successful reproduction.

As we set out to search for the Flamingoes we found ourselves in the vicinity of the Zoological Park on the outskirts of Les Saintes Maries, and we decided to pay it a visit. If we failed to find Flamingoes in the wild we should at least have seen them in a setting as closely approximating to the wild as aviary conditions would allow. The Flamingo pool was, in fact, very pleasantly contrived, and the birds in fine plumage. Other Camargue birds – Little Egrets, Purple Herons, Black-winged Stilts and various other wader species – were not so happily placed, and the mammals – badgers, foxes and wild boars – were in very cramped quarters.

We resumed our quest for the Flamingoes on the Étang de Vaccares, following a rough road that flanked its western shore. Binoculars were held in readiness, and it was not long before we glimpsed a distant line of rose-pink and white birds half a mile out in the shallows. Some six hundred birds were feeding there, and we viewed them with the greatest satisfaction.

Two other car-loads of bird-watchers also stopped at the roadside, and, in their eagerness to get a clearer view, several of the keener types began striding across the salicornia marsh towards the water's edge. This precipitated a positively indecent rush by all concerned. A stream of humanity went surging across the hundred yards of green marsh, and had the Flamingoes not been a very long way away, they must surely have taken fright at such a violent and unwarranted invasion of their domain.

On the return journey we traversed a wilderness of reeds above which, cleaving the air in great curving arcs, were seven scythe-winged Falcons. The sudden warmth of this April afternoon must have brought an unusual richness of insect life winging from the reed beds. These slaty-grey Falcons with chestnut underparts were Hobbies pursuing their prey. They were feeding voraciously. Again and again, without any check in speed, a bird would reach forward with outstretched talons to snatch a seemingly invisible object from the air, and then, with a quick lowering of the head, transfer it from claw to bill. Scarcely larger than a Kestrel, the Hobby must be, for its size, one of the fastest flyers in the world of birds. Hobbies have even been seen pursuing and overtaking Swifts in flight, nonchalantly plucking them out of the sky in passing. These birds that we were now watching would, in a short time, be moving northwards to their breeding-sites. A few Hobbies cross the Channel and nest in England, usually south of the Thames, though occasionally further north. My earliest acquaintance with these birds was made with a pair that nested within easy cycling distance of Cambridge.

When we sniffed the air the following morning we were fairly certain that a change of weather was imminent. A fitful sun was still shining, but a cold air-stream was sweeping down the Rhône valley – the Mistral was about to set in. We decided to go inland for the day to explore Roman Provence – Nîmes, the Pont du Gard and Tarascon. We arrived back at Arles in the late afternoon, but could not resist an evening sortie to the Étang de Vaccares to see it in Mistral conditions. Against a ruddy sunset the reed beds were leaning in the wind, and Little Egrets were struggling to their roost with some difficulty in the gathering gloom. We were up at six the following morning to pay a last visit to the reserve, and we added Woodchat Shrike to our bird list. We paid a brief visit of farewell to the Biological Station, filmed some of the birds in the pens there – mostly 'cripples' from the marshes being brought back to health and strength. We had a brief 'Ave et Vale' with Dr. Luc Hoffman, and then returned to the caravan to make preparations for an after-lunch departure. In our five days in the Camargue we could do no more than sample the delights that it had to offer, but we felt that we had used the time well, and for four days out of five the weather had been superb. The onset of Mistral conditions on our last day made it comparatively easy to wrench ourselves away. Honesty compels me to admit that we were, in fact, quite relieved to be flying north – for warmth and respite from the wind. Besides, our permits to visit 'Les Sept Îles' on the Atlantic coast had arrived. In the limited time available it should be just possible to have an excursion to the celebrated 'Bird Rocks of Brittany' – the first bird sanctuary to be created in France, and well deserving a visit.

4

North to Belgium

THE archipelago of 'Les Sept Îles' lies some three to
six miles off the coast of Brittany. It is estimated that
on the main islands of Rouzic, Malban and Le Cerf about
thirty thousand Puffins breed annually, together with
three thousand Guillemots, six to eight hundred Razorbills, and gulls innumerable. There are also breeding
Choughs and Ravens, Peregrine Falcons, Cormorants
and Shags, Storm Petrels, and a few Oyster-catchers and
Common Terns. But perhaps the most interesting of all
the birds there are the newly-arrived Gannets. This is
the most southerly breeding-station of 'Sula bassana'.
Thirty-five years ago the first Gannets were seen
prospecting Rouzic. In 1939 about twenty couples nested
on top of the island. Then came the war years and a
consequent and welcome isolation from which they
greatly benefited. At the end of hostilities some hundred
pairs were nesting on Rouzic. Today, about two
thousand Gannets are nesting there, and their future
appears safe in the capable hands of the French equivalent of the R.S.P.B., the L.P.O. (La Ligue Française
pour la Protection des Oiseaux).

At the turn of the century, however, a very different
state of affairs prevailed on these islands. As early as

1878, Dr. Louis Bureau, Director of the Natural History Museum at Nantes, had warned his fellow countrymen that unless the wanton and senseless slaughter of Puffins and other sea fowl was stopped, these islands would be totally denuded of their breeding birds. The full horror of the situation, however, was only revealed later by the publication of a letter written by Lt. Hémery to Dr. Bureau after a visit to Rouzic in June, 1911. 'A first impression of the Puffins on the island of Rouzic,' he wrote, 'was of a colony rather thin in numbers. What an understatement! The colony had been decimated: the island had the appearance of a veritable battlefield. Outside the burrows where the birds rear their young were blow-flies, and everywhere there was the stench of corruption. Lying in heaps on the ground were hundreds of empty cartridges – like the used bullet-cases from a machine-gun after a battle. We extracted from the burrows young Puffins, dead these six or seven days. We removed eggs deserted and rotten. We found only one adult female in an occupied nesting-hole, and another close to a nine- or ten-day-old chick. We then learnt from some boatmen that eight days previous, two or three 'sportsmen' arrived from Paris, and were landed on the island with a crate of cartridges weighing over a hundredweight. They did not leave the island until they had discharged every single cartridge at these harmless birds, slaughtering them as they returned to their nests with food for their young. The corpses of their victims were taken to Perros and dumped on the beach. Proud of their bag these Sporting Gentlemen returned with only an odd bird or two as personal trophies. It seems that these same vandals carry out these useless and stupid massacres almost every year. We can foresee that under these circumstances the Puffin colony at Rouzic will, in three or four years' time, have been completely wiped out.'

Action followed the publication of this trenchant document. The L.P.O. was founded in 1912, and its first achievement was to safeguard the Puffins of Rouzic. Thus was born the first 'Reserve ornithologique' of France. Seventeen years later the L.P.O. succeeded in extending the protected area to include the neighbouring islands of Malban, Plate and L'Île aux Rats, and also two rocky outcrops which have been honoured with the name 'island' to make up the total to seven. Since then many coastal cliff areas on the mainland have been given sanctuary status. Brittany intends to preserve its sea-birds for future generations to enjoy. We were delighted at the prospect of visiting some of these reserves, but would the weather make this possible?

We battled up the Rhône valley in the teeth of the wind. A night-stop at Loriel brought little comfort. An American caravanning party newly arrived from Western Germany reported coming through snow on their way down. The following morning as we climbed the Mont du Beaujolais heading west from Lyons we ourselves encountered snow in drifts on the roadsides when in thick mist we topped the Col du Pin Blanc, before dropping down to the valley of the Loire and the château country. We passed the night at Lapalisse and went on to Moulins the following morning through cherry orchards where the road verges were sprinkled with cowslips. We had a lunch stop at Bourges so that we could visit the cathedral and see its incomparable stained glass. Then on through Ramorantin where a dead Heron, being used as a bird-scarer, lay hideously spread-eagled over a cottage garden. A pleasant lake and woodland stretch followed, but we were hurrying westwards and paused only to note a dead polecat, an unusual traffic casualty, flattened on the road. This was not the only mammal corpse that we saw on this busy stretch of road. Several hedgehogs had met with disaster, and two domestic cats. We had already noted the high mortality rate of cats on the highways of France where the Citroen and the Pugeot now rank as its natural predators.

We halted for the night at Beuré, and at dawn had Serin Finches singing in the trees and making Green-finch-like display-flights between the trees and the telephone wires on the roadside. Starlings had now reappeared – the first that we had seen since viewing with some dismay an aviary crowded with these birds at the Zoological Park at Les Saintes Maries. The Starling is so common in England that it comes as a surprise to find that in France it is a comparative rarity in the southern half of the country – sufficiently unusual in the Camargue to merit aviary status.

From Beuré we progressed steadily north-west into Brittany, and, during a brief sunny interval, we stopped for half an hour in a bluebell wood a few miles beyond Laval. A Wryneck was calling. Wood Warblers, Willow Warblers and Chiffchaffs were all in full song, and Brimstone and Orange Tip butterflies were on the wing – an idyllic setting for lunch – apart from the wood ants, a fiery breed, that sensed the presence of un-desirable aliens on Gallic soil, and reacted accordingly with a remarkable display of patriotic fervour. Ruefully rubbing our nether regions we resumed our journey to the Atlantic coast. Cowslips now gave way to primroses on the roadside banks. We were coming under the influence of the warm, wet westerlies. And so, in the late afternoon, we came down the long estuary of the River Rance to St. Malo. Tomorrow we would spend exploring the coast of Brittany with a visit to Les Sept Îles in prospect for Monday – if the weather improved. But we had our doubts. Rain squalls and brilliant bursts of sunshine had been alternating all day long, with the wind increasing steadily from the west.

But first we must book passages for our wives and the children to return to England as soon as could conveniently be arranged. An inquiry at the Syndicat d'Initiative for details of the sailing times of the St. Malo–Southampton boat was met with a look of blank incredulity. We might as well have been inquiring at Plymouth for the Mayflower's next voyage to the Americas. The St. Malo–Southampton service had long since been suspended. There were flights from Dinard, or sailings from Cherbourg, but, from St. Malo – nothing.

It was a very dispirited party that settled down for the night in camp-site 'Aleth' on the outskirts of the town, in the lee of a vast concrete fortress that had formed part of the Atlantic Wall. The following morning, inquiries at Dinard airport were not encouraging. The weather in Jersey was very bad. Flights were being delayed or cancelled. Gales were forecast. The possibility of visiting Les Sept Îles, six miles out in the Atlantic, in an open boat, now receded to vanishing point. The all-important thing now was to get our wives and the children safely to a port within easy reach of home – and that meant Cherbourg or Dieppe. We studied the maps, and there, half-way to Dieppe, we noticed the little town of Bayeux. Why, of course, the Tapestry! That decided us, so towards Bayeux we went, and camped the night at St. Lo. We were now in Normandy. Just across the Channel lay England – and it was raining. But the Bayeux Tapestry was splendid. Its state of preservation and its manner of display were most impressive. Disappointment over Les Sept Îles visit was receding. We sped northwards, through Arromanches where the concrete caissons out at sea still serve as a grim reminder of 'D' Day, 1944. With the Bayeux Tapestry still fresh in the memory, it was interesting to reflect that we had encountered the visible evidence of two invasions – separated by nine hundred years – in one day's travel through wet and windy Normandy. At Pont l'Evêque we stopped to buy cheeses. At Rouen we drew off into the municipal caravan site, but promptly drew out again when beset by dogs, noise and litter, and decided to press on to Dieppe which we reached as darkness fell. We camped in howling wind and rain under the shelter of a high wall that we prayed would not fall over and crush us during the night. But towards dawn the wind moderated. The gale was blowing itself out. By mid-morning the wind had dropped completely, and, when the sun broke through, a reasonably comfortable Channel crossing seemed assured. We could say our farewells 'sans peur et sans reproche'. The long, weary hours of travel were forgotten: the St. Malo fiasco was forgiven. 'Au revoir nos femmes! Bon voyage, mes petites!' We watched the cross-Channel ferry recede into the blue distance. For the next two months we should be fending for ourselves. From now onwards it was 'Northward Ho! – Men only' – a sobering thought, particularly when one considered the preparation and disposal of two months of meals. But the die was cast. There was no going back now.

5

Belgian Reserves –
Le Blankaart and Le Zwin

WE HAD five hours of daylight in which to make as much progress as we could towards the Belgian border which we hoped to cross the following morning. Edgard Kesteloot, Secretary-General of the administrative council that conserves nature reserves in Belgium, had arranged a very full programme for us during the few days that we should be passing through his country, and it was advisable to arrive on time. From Dieppe we travelled over the wolds, the roadside trees gradually changing from black poplars to beeches, elms and limes. Rooks had reappeared as familiar farmland birds. Quite suddenly, from St. Omer to Dunkirk, we found ourselves in a Flemish landscape of dyke-intersected meadows flanked by pollarded willows, where sluggish canals meandered across the flat countryside. We stopped for the night at Malo-sur-Mer just outside Dunkirk on a camp-site on the edge of the dunes – the same dunes in which thousands of our countrymen had sheltered during that historic week of hasty evacuation from the near-by beaches in the early summer of 1940.

We spent a cold night at Dunkirk – a night of heavy rain that beat a tattoo on the caravan roof unceasingly

through the hours of darkness. But the weather cheered
up a little at dawn, and an optimistic Cuckoo kept calling
and insisting that it wasn't such a bad day as April days
go, and it was high time we were stirring. We were on
the road by 9 a.m. and soon crossed over into Belgium
where we were immediately conscious of a rather formal
and decidedly more serious atmosphere. The landscape
was tidy: the road verges were trimly kept: the people
had a serious demeanour, and they were more warmly
and more soberly dressed. Even the cows in the fields
had sacking overcoats to shield them from the wind.
The countryside was decidedly Flemish: the faces often
strikingly 'Breughel'.

What did we know about this country that we were
about to explore – its size, and the density of its population, and the pressures on its wildlife? Belgium is only
an eighth the size of Great Britain. It is in fact not much
larger than Wales, but its nine million people are seven
hundred to the square mile compared to our five hundred
and forty. But, as we were to discover, it still has many
unspoilt areas of great natural beauty, and an awareness
of their value and of the need for conservation. The
Royal Institute of Natural Sciences co-ordinates conservation work in the country, and a great many reserves
are under the aegis of the R.N.O.B. (Reserves Naturelles
et Ornithologiques de Belgique), including Le Blankaart,
Chenal de l'Yser and Le Zwin, all of which we hoped to
visit. It would have been pleasant to have included
Bruyère de Kalmthout, a heath and woodland reserve,
in our itinerary, but it was some distance inland and
would have involved a wide détour. In recent years
there has been a strong movement in Belgium towards

the creation of numerous small reserves – little copses, patches of scrubland, heath or marsh – where a 'collaborateur' keeps an eye on things.

We camped in a pleasant well-kept site on the outskirts of Nieuwpoort, where we sauntered along the quay and watched the fishermen cleaning up their boats after the night's catch. In the afternoon we had a rendezvous at Le Blankaart, Woumen, a few miles inland where we were to meet the Warden and be shown over the reserve.

Le Blankaart is a gracious château rebuilt forty years ago after its destruction in the First World War. Originally a private residence, it is now a Volkshogeschool or 'Folk High School' on the Danish pattern, with distinct similarities to the Adult Education Centres in rural England. It combines the running of cultural courses for adults with the conservation of an extensive area of lake and marshland, formerly the shooting preserve of the family living in the château. It stands in parkland, the breeding haunt of several pairs of Golden Orioles, and it overlooks a watery wilderness of reed beds and swamp. Two of the few duck decoys in Belgium are sited there, and though both have fallen into disuse, there is a strong possibility of at least one of them being brought into use again for 'ringing' purposes as part of the conservation programme.

As a ringing station Le Blankaart has a very impressive record, thanks to the enthusiasm of the Warden, Paul Houwen, who greeted us cordially on our arrival, and was soon conducting us on a tour of the reserve. 'Mist-nets' were cunningly concealed – as I found to my cost – at vantage points along the paths that led to the lake. We had not walked twenty yards before I found myself hopelessly enmeshed. I only hope that it will not go down in the official record that the first capture of the afternoon was a stupid Englishman who, with open eyes, walked head first into a net that promptly seized every available button on his person, and from which he was extracted with some difficulty and a good deal of leg-pulling on the part of his Belgian host. After this contretemps we walked more warily, and, in the next hundred yards, extracted from the nets a Sedge Warbler, a Blue-headed Wagtail and a Blackbird; and then three young Mallards from a wader trap by the water's edge. We were also shown a Musk Rat trapped earlier in the day. From the osier beds came a 'reeling' song similar to a Grasshopper Warbler's but less sustained – a Savi's Warbler's, a new species for us.

Paul Houwen combined an accurate knowledge of the birds in his reserve with a delightful enthusiasm for his work as conservationist and bird-ringer. The previous year he had ringed 5,200 birds of 105 species at Le Blankaart, mostly by mist-netting in daytime, but a great many in the reed beds at night by torchlight. It takes courage as well as enthusiasm to pounce on a Bittern that is being held in the beam of a torch at night-time. We questioned him about bird protection in general in his country. He said there was not yet the same feeling for birds in Belgium as in England. There was, however, a growing interest in reserves, and a lot of concern by a minority of his countrymen for the protection of rarer species. Although legislation was being prepared to put an end to it, there was still an appalling massacre of passerine birds in Belgium each autumn. From the first to the fifteenth of November trapping was still permitted by law and had come to be regarded almost as a national sport. Every November about fifteen million – note, fifteen million! – Thrushes and Blackbirds, Larks and Linnets, Finches and Buntings were caught in nets and traps. Most of these were killed and dispatched to Paris to be served up in hotels and restaurants as delicacies for Parisian gourmets. Finches, Linnets and other birds considered suitable for caging were destined for the cage-bird trade. The trapping of small birds for food was not allowed in France, but the hoteliers and restaurateurs were only too happy to import them from a neighbouring country.

'We are behind the times, compared with England,' said Paul Houwen. 'But not by many years,' we reminded him. It is not so very long ago that plump Wheatears, on autumn migration, were trapped by shepherds on the South Downs in staggering numbers, and sent to the poulterers' shops in Brighton and Eastbourne to satisfy the jaded palates of gourmets there. Twenty-two thousand Wheatears was an ordinary seasonal catch for the Eastbourne district alone.

There was also the lucrative business of decoying and netting song-birds. Present bird-lovers in the south of England, gladdened by the sight of an occasional Goldfinch in their gardens, may be surprised to learn that at one time over fifteen thousand Goldfinches were caught annually on the thistle-strewn downland slopes behind the town of Worthing. After a particularly successful season the market for song-birds became glutted. 'Then might be seen in the streets of the coastal towns the juvenile members of the bird-catching fraternity hawking their wares to passers-by – bouquets of dead Goldfinches tied up with Yellow Wagtails, Green-finches and Linnets in variegated bundles from which their heads protruded like ripe berries.'

'Lark-spinning' on the downs was also a profitable occupation. A large 'mushroom', on the rounded top of which were embedded pieces of mirror glass, was rotated on a spindle by a distant cord. This glittering object held a deadly fascination for Skylarks passing over the downs on frosty mornings. As they hovered over the fateful spot the guns would blaze away. In January 1877, the hosts of Midian prowling over the downs just behind Brighton accounted for twelve thousand larks in a single morning. At least we have put an end to barbaric practices such as these. It is gratifying to record that not long after our visit to Belgium legislation was passed by the Belgian government drastically curtailing the autumn trade in netted song-birds. The legislation was passed in the teeth of bitter opposition. There were rowdy protest marches, and Edgard Kesteloot, Head of Conservation, was burned in effigy by his outraged countrymen.

After our visit to Le Blankaart we arranged with Paul Houwen to pay a visit on the following morning to a new tidal estuary reserve – the Chenal de l'Yser – north of the river at Nieuwpoort.

It was a grey morning with a cold wind and a threat of rain in the air as we followed our guide down the river bank. Lapwings were nesting in the nearby fields, and several pairs of Kentish Plovers were settling into breeding territories. The reserve area is a stretch of tidal mud and rough shoreline on the northern side of this busy, industrial river. The reserve serves principally as a refuge for migrating waders. We saw Curlew, Knot, Sanderling and Dunlin there, and had a memorable view of five Grey Plovers in their black and silver breeding dress. 'A very goot observation,' said the enthusiastic Paul – a saying we were to cherish for future use. A few waders breed in the reserve, Lapwings, Kentish Plovers and Oyster-catchers – the latter occasionally on the flat roofs of war-time concrete bunkers built by the German forces for estuary defence. Paul also pointed out a large mooring-post in the river itself, on the top of which a pair of Oyster-catchers reared a family last year. The first female Yellow Wagtails appeared this morning – the colourful males had arrived a week before. By the end of our walk along the river bank a steady rain had set in, and we returned to the car thoroughly drenched. We had entertained hopes of a return to Le Blankaart for an exploration of the duck decoys and reed beds, but the sensible plan now was to return Paul to his home, and for us to make for the caravan to dry off and to change our clothes. We said farewell to Paul and were glad to seek the warmth of the caravan for the rest of the day. Tomorrow, wet or fine, we were due at Le Zwin.

We awoke early to find – wonder of wonders – a windless morning and a cloudless sky. It was a pity not to see the Chenal de l'Yser under more favourable conditions, so we paid a pre-breakfast visit there, and were rewarded with some excellent views of waders on the estuarine mud at low tide – Bar-tailed Godwits and Curlews in strength, and a scattering of smaller waders for good measure. Early morning mists were rolling in as we returned to the caravan, and it was in a mist-shrouded world that we made our way up the Belgian coast to-wards Knokke and the Dutch border. As we neared Le Zwin the sun broke through and we knew that we were in for a glorious day.

Le Zwin, which lies a short distance up the coast from Knokke, is a Belgian counterpart of the Severn Wildfowl Trust at Slimbridge. It is the creation of Count Lippens, Mayor of Knokke, and we found it fascinating not only because of its delightful setting but because of the con-servation projects that are being undertaken there. It conserves a large area of marsh and dune, formerly a royal shooting preserve but now a sanctuary where Avocets and Oyster-catchers, Shelducks and Mallard breed undisturbed, and where migrating waders can find sanctuary. Mallards and their ducklings were scampering about near the turnstiles at the entrance, and Collared Doves were scarcely to be disturbed by passers-by as they trotted about the walk-ways. Tree Sparrows were abundant and were everywhere usurping nesting-boxes no doubt originally intended for tits.

On approaching the public entrance we were met by a smiling official who declined to take the proffered entrance fee and who immediately conducted us into the studio-office of the Warden, Th. Robyns de Schneidauer – 'Peter Robyns' – who was expecting us in readiness for a tour of the reserve.

I retain the happiest memories of the next hour or two that we spent in his company. First of all we crossed a marsh from which a score of Avocets leapt into the air before proceeding to police us off their territory with urgent 'kluit . . . kluit' cries. We then moved across a slightly elevated sandy area riddled with rabbit holes from which half a dozen Jackdaws and a Stock Dove hastily emerged on hearing our footsteps. We were told that Shelducks, Little Owls and Starlings also use these rabbit holes for nesting purposes. There is an acute housing shortage on this open terrain for birds that need a cavity in which to rear their young.

From the underground Jackdaw colony we made our way towards an island set in the middle of an area of flooded saltings. At our approach a host of Black-headed Gulls took to the air, brawling and squawking in protest. Some two thousand gulls nest on the island, and we were able to take some distant ciné shots of them as they returned to their nests.

We continued across the marsh, conscious now of a continual movement of birds in the sky above that was quite unrelated to the clamour of the gullery through which we had passed. All the time as we traversed the reserve a steady wader migration was in progress overhead. A party of Greenshanks came winging over with excited 'tew...tew...tew' cries. Scarcely were they out of sight than the air vibrated with the 'titti...titti...titti' calls of Whimbrel heading north. Spotted Redshanks in twos and threes came hurtling past, their loud, clear 'chewit...chewit' cries immediately revealing their identity. Bar-tailed Godwits, less vocal but travelling in larger parties, came speeding by, their russet breasts showing clearly in the bright sunlight. 'They, at least, are through safely,' said Peter Robyns. 'Tomorrow, in France, the great massacre begins.' We asked him to explain. He told us how the French authorities allow an 'open' season for shore-shooting from the first to the fifteenth of May. It is designed to coincide with the peak period of wader migration. For a fortnight, thousands of guns are blazing away all down the coastline of France at anything resembling a wader that is passing through. Dunlins, Sanderlings, Turnstones and Sandpipers are all considered fair game, as well as the larger waders – the Whimbrel, 'Shankers' and Godwits that we were watching now. All must run the gauntlet to provide sport for the trigger-happy shore-gunners.

At the north end of the marshes at Le Zwin is a tidal creek up which floats flotsam and jetsam from the nearby sea. We were soon to see another example of the ravages wrought by man – albeit unintentionally in this instance – on the birds that share the world with him. Along the banks of this tidal creek was a sordid accumulation of the litter that civilized man in the mid-twentieth century leaves in his wake – planks and bottles and polythene containers, and all of them smeared with oil. And, floating in the tideway, were the bodies of seabirds – Guillemots and Razorbills, Scoters and Divers – helpless victims of oil pollution. Peter Robyns had collected together a heap of these pathetic, oil-sodden bundles. 'Every year it is the same,' he said. 'In spite of legislation we see no improvement. It is one of the most serious problems of our time.' In our own country the Torrey Canyon disaster has highlighted for us the appalling consequences of oil pollution for the seabirds in our coastal waters. But this is no new problem. It has been going on for a long time. Thirty years ago one could reckon on finding a score of seabird corpses on a five-mile walk along the shores of Liverpool Bay. One wonders how long the seabird population of the western world can stand this drain on their breeding population.

Will the Guillemot and the Razorbill eventually follow the Great Auk into final extinction?

We began our return journey over the marsh, and soon re-entered the kingdom of the 'Black-heads' – an area of tussocky grass where an overspill population of gulls crowded out from the island colony was breeding. Many nests already contained eggs, and we had to be careful where we placed our feet. In the general disturbance resulting from our invasion we might have missed seeing seven Black Terns, on migration, that suddenly appeared flying overhead. These dark, slaty-grey birds with a beautifully buoyant flight were promptly mobbed by the gulls and emphatically shown off the premises and dispatched on their way north.

This lovely area of marshland had one further surprise in store. As we walked over a particularly squelchy patch of bogland, a bird unmistakably snipe-like but most surprisingly large, suddenly and silently leapt up from our feet, zigzagged a short distance ahead of us, and dropped back into the marsh. Stealthily we moved forward, and again it leapt up from our feet – huge and snipelike, with white showing at the sides of its tail.

There could be no doubt about it. We were all looking at our first Great Snipe, one of the most elusive waders on the British – or, for that matter, on the Belgian List. The bird books describe it as 'a very scarce passage-migrant' which means, as far as Britain is concerned, that you may spend a whole lifetime looking out for unusual migrants and still not see a Great Snipe. This bird would be on its way to its breeding grounds in the vast, marshy wildernesses of northern Norway, Sweden or Finland, where it would soon be indulging in those strange communal courtship rites that make this bird's display so fascinating for the few who have been privileged to witness it. The display begins in the twilight and continues until the approach of dawn when the midnight revellers go their several ways in pairs to the hidden swamps where, in due course, their families will be reared.

In the south corner of the Zwin reserve is an extensive shallow pool ideally suited to the feeding needs of Avocets. A permanent hide is sited by the water's edge, and Peter Robyns took us there and installed us within. It was not long before half a dozen Avocets, feeding busily with side-to-side sweeps of their upturned bills, were working steadily nearer. The striking pattern of black barrings on snow-white plumage makes this distinguished member of the wader family unmistakable. Until a century and a half ago the Avocet was a familiar bird in East Anglia and the Lincolnshire fenlands, but intensive drainage and constant persecution finally drove it away. Its memory lingers on in place-names. Near Crowland is a signpost to Kluit, a remote hamlet in the fens. 'Kluit…kluit…kluit' is the Avocet's call-note, and Kluit is the Dutch name for this bird. Now, after the lapse of a century or more, the Avocet has returned to our shores. The colonies in Holland, where an enlightened people afford the bird full protection, appear to be sending over their surplus to East Anglia. In the summer of 1947, in two adjacent localities on the east coast, small colonies of Avocets established themselves. Under the aegis of the R.S.P.B. the birds are now thoroughly established and are prospering. Havergate Island in Suffolk is now a place of pilgrimage for bird-watchers from all over Britain, and the effective measures being taken to afford these lovely birds security from their natural enemies, and from those miserable klepto-maniacs the egg-collectors, and from the irresponsible man with a gun, are reaping their reward.

Shelducks, also strikingly black and white, but with chestnut around their fore-parts, and with splendid red, ceiling-wax knobs on their bills, also arrived within photographic range. Common Terns, on migration, kept alighting on posts specially sited in the water at a convenient photographic range of four or five yards' distance. Redshanks picked their way delicately along the water's edge, and passed in front of the hide a mere three feet away. Cameras were kept busily clicking. Film went whizzing merrily through the ciné camera. It was a very happy hour.

So far we had not properly inspected the main wild-fowl collection, and we felt it was time to remedy this omission. As soon as we entered the area where the main collections were housed we were conscious of excellence in all that we saw. There was an air of spaciousness about the place, and evidence everywhere of care and concern. Scrupulous cleanliness of the pens was observable, and the birds were in immaculate plumage. As at Slimbridge there were ducks of every conceivable species, and geese too, though the emphasis here was on the Greylag. In former years Greylags bred in the wild in Belgium. Le Zwin hopes by its breeding successes within the reserve eventually to repopulate Belgium with Greylag Geese. Already there were some two hundred Greylags breeding there. It was splendid to see proud parents accompanied by five or six golden goslings, and to find this repopulation project proceeding very satisfactorily in its initial stages. The other birds that immediately came to one's notice were the Storks. Very rarely in the past have Storks bred successfully in captivity or semi-captivity. Here at Le Zwin a pinioned Stork mated to a free-flying bird had built a nest on the ground, completely disregarding some attractively-sited cartwheels and platforms at a higher level. Eggs had been laid and incubation was in progress. We watched a ceremonial 'change-over' of duties, and filmed the male bird bringing additional nesting material from the marshes some distance away.

Another very interesting feature of Le Zwin were the wader pens. These little mud-trotters and dabblers in the tidal ooze require, in spite of their chosen habitat, scrupulous cleanliness in their environment. At Le Zwin the art of wader management has been brought near to perfection. It has been recognized from the start that they have special requirements. Waders require damp conditions underfoot with abundant herbage constantly sprayed, and flowering plants to attract insects. They need water in which to dabble, but this must be under control and never allowed to become fouled. Here, the cement runnels in which they paddle are scrubbed out three times a week. Most of all they require the right food. After a lot of experiment it was discovered that waders get on very well on a diet of chicken guts cleaned and chopped up into worm-size portions.

We found the Ruff and Reeve pen particularly interesting. Here a score of these birds were indulging in exactly the same fantastic, quasi-pugilistic display in the middle of the pen as were their free-flying cousins in the nearby marshes. And the Reeves, after pairing, actually nest in the herbage round the edge of the pen. In an adjacent enclosure for large waders a Black-tailed God-wit also nested in the herbage a year ago, and we could well understand how this could happen, for while we were there many of the birds were so full of well-being that display was taking place. Their wild, clear courtship calls were ringing out, and there was every sign that they had similar intentions this year – but – and this is the splendid thing about it – it would be a different pair of Godwits, for with very few exceptions the waders are released from their captive state each year in early October. They are set free during the autumn migration: they rejoin their fellows on the mud-flats and wing their way south. They have been put to the inconvenience of temporary captivity at Le Zwin. Now they may fly free once more. One or two must be detained to teach next season's newcomers their table manners. Experience has shown that Redshanks have a flair for passing on feeding information: in the wader world they are Nature's 'schoolmasters', and so one or two must forego their liberty in consequence.

We questioned Peter Robyns on the question of wader numbers, particularly of birds passing through at migra-tion time. He expressed a deep concern over the sharp decline he had noted in wader numbers during the spring migration. The previous autumn there had been a strong passage south following what had clearly been a good breeding-season in the high north. But something was happening to the birds either in their winter quarters, or on their return journey in the early spring. This was particularly noticeable with the small waders like

Dunlins that frequent estuarine mud. Could it be that chemical effluents from factories were contaminating the mud and poisoning the organisms on which the birds feed? Or were the rivers now beginning to bring down higher concentrations of pesticide residues leached from farmlands? It is an inescapable fact that every river ultimately derives its water from a thousand rivulets and streams that result, directly or indirectly, from land drainage. But whatever the cause, the effects are becoming more and more evident. Every year there are fewer waders hastening north at breeding time.

The following day – the First of May – was 'Socialist Day' in Belgium and a general holiday. Edgard Kesteloot had advised us to avoid the vicinity of holiday resorts and places of popular appeal, so we decided to explore the relatively unfrequented dune area north of Le Zwin and just over the Dutch border. We wanted to see visible migration in progress, and, in particular, to watch waders streaming north along the coast.

The sea-buckthorn thickets on the edges of the dunes were full of small birds on the move, including Nightingales that gave occasional bursts of song. From a patch of elders a spectacular black and orange-yellow bird shot out before our startled eyes – a male Golden Oriole – 'a very goot observation'.

But we also wanted to experience migration on a more intimate scale, and a carefully chosen place behind the shelter of the sea-wall afforded this, for quite apart from the waders that were winging past fairly high in the air, another passage of birds was taking place a few feet above our heads. Singly, and in twos and threes, they came streaming past – Swallows, Martins and

Swifts – an endless flow of birds. It was not that we were overwhelmed by numbers. At no time were there more than a score of birds in our field of vision, but it was the sheer, unflagging persistence of this northward passage that was so impressive. An entire population was shifting north: a whole nation was on the move.

A little further up the coast we found a reedy mere where twenty Avocets, half a dozen Ruffs and a score of Garganeys were feeding. From the top of the sea wall we scanned the ploughland surrounding the mere and immediately noted four Avocets sitting on nests. With their startlingly black and white plumage they were painfully visible at a great distance against that background of dark brown earth from which the first green spears of corn were sprouting. One might suppose that a bird with plumage as conspicuous as an Avocet's would be visible at a great distance whatever its background. We were to find at a later stage of our journey that this was not so. In the Netherlands we were to come across a colony of Avocets in partially flooded rough pasture where the gleam of sky on watery patches in the grassland provided perfect camouflage. At a range of less than a hundred yards a dozen birds sitting out there in the open were practically invisible.

It had been suggested that we might visit the De Braakman reserve later in the afternoon. A very considerable lake, an offshoot of the Wester Schelde estuary, forms the heart of the reserve. We were immediately reminded of the Norfolk Broads, for the lake is open for sailing and there was the pleasant spectacle of a score of yachts criss-crossing its placid surface. Woodlands and reed beds surrounded the lake and access to these was limited, and close to the yachting station was an area of quaking marsh completely given over to the birds. It was only a few acres in extent and yachts were constantly sailing past, but it was packed with birds. Black-headed Gulls were nesting, Avocets and Redshanks were plentiful, and there was even a Ruff's tilting-ground. Oyster-catchers were piping, and colourful Sheldrakes conversing in nasal tones. Everywhere there was evidence of a most thriving community of marsh and water birds – and all made possible by a little forethought on the part of conservationists, and by a sensible and responsible attitude by all who used the lake for recreational purposes. In countries like Belgium and Holland with high population densities, compromises like this must be accepted as part of conservation policy. The eminently satisfactory situation at De Braakman shows that it can be made to work.

6

Birds in the 'Vaterland'

Before we penetrated too deeply into this new country some consideration should be given to the unusual geographical situation in which the peoples of the Netherlands find themselves, with half their country below sea-level, and nearly a sixth of it actually under water. Paradoxically, this country we were now entering was the most densely populated in Europe. Its twelve million people occupied their 16,800 square miles of territory at a density of over 1,000 to the square mile, compared with 270 in France, 540 in Great Britain and 700 in Belgium. The question that interested us was would there be any room in this crowded country for wildlife haunts and habitats? The answer, we were to discover, was decidedly in the affirmative. Some of the finest 'wetlands' reserves in Europe are to be found in Holland where areas of marsh defeat even a Dutchman's skill and ingenuity in draining water from the land. Reclamation is always taking place, and the enclosure and draining of much of the former Zuyder Zee, and the new Delta-plan in the south-west will eventually add significantly to the country's habitable area. The problem of keeping the sea at bay is an ever-present one, and the tragic consequences of storm and tide combining together in an assault on the defences – as happened in 1952 – are still fresh in the memory. The sea with its hidden menace is always there behind the dunes, and even under normal conditions there is usually more water in the low-lying hinterland than can satisfactorily be pumped or drained away. Some inland areas are permanently sodden and waterlogged, and there are 'polders' where the peaty ground shudders under one's footfall, and where a false step can mean a sudden immersion thigh-deep into sour brown water. Such places, unprofitable for farming, are often converted into nature sanctuaries, and it is there that so many species of birds delightful to an Englishman's eyes because so rare in his own country are to be encountered. Not surprisingly Holland has the smallest area of forest in any country in Europe. Its wealth of wildlife lies in its 'wetlands'.

The Dutch have always taken a lead in conservation matters. In this densely populated country many problems are constantly arising over the protection of natural resources. The Netherlands government, supported by many private organizations, frequently introduces legislation to resolve these difficulties. Of the private organizations 'The Society for the Conservation of Nature Reserves in the Netherlands' is one of the most influential. It owns and manages some eighty reserves and is all the time seeking to create additional ones. Each of the eleven provinces of the Netherlands possesses its own 'County Naturalists Trusts', and between them they manage reserves totalling over five thousand acres. Another private organization called 'The Foundation for Nature Protection' owns a total of seven thousand-three hundred acres, including four important national parks. The Netherlands Society for the Protection of Birds actively encourages the study and protection of birds as does its counterpart in Britain. Altogether some three hundred and fifty square miles of the Netherlands – a thirty-fifth of its total surface area – is 'protected' in one way or another. It is true to say that in no other country in Europe is a greater concern shown for the plant and animal communities that share tenure of the land with man. It is worthy of mention, too, that in the Netherlands, where preoccupation with drainage is a national necessity, there should be a concern for the dispossessed – for frogs and toads and newts that would disappear almost in toto if drainage schemes were always as successful as their sponsors intended them to be. In the Netherlands there are a few small but very special reserves for amphibians. For them every acre of drained fenland means deprivation and the loss of their ancestral home, and this is on the Dutch conscience. To redress the balance is impossible, but a gesture has been made.

As we journeyed through southern Holland the dominant bird was clearly the Black-headed Gull. Everywhere the search for food was taking place – we disturbed one pecking at a hedgehog corpse that lay squashed on the road – not a pretty sight. We skirted Antwerp and drew off the road at Oosterhout and into a gloomy pine wood on the edge of an army tank-range. It rained all night and in the sodden darkness outside the caravan a Long-eared Owl moaned and complained – at least that was the impression given by those tremulous, mournful notes that went on hour by hour. In fact it was the bird's springtime courtship call. Out of the breeding season the Long-eared Owl is the most silent of birds. We were glad when daylight came and that low, sighing 'oo-oo-oo' ceased, and we could leave the gloom of the pine woods and resume our journey across the flat acres of Noord Brabant. We passed Biesbosch, haunt of Spoon-bills, above the Hollandsch Diep, and saw a distant white 'heron' that must have been a Spoonbill. On again, through little villages where elderly cottagers wearing yellow wooden sabots were pottering about in their tidy cottage gardens. And so to Amsterdam, the weather clearing, and through the dock area to the northern suburbs and thence by a narrow coastal road through old Holland by the Zuyder Zee to Ouitdam, and a water-logged caravan site on a neck of land wrested from the Ijsselmeer, and so low-lying that one suffered all the time from an uneasy feeling of being permanently below the level of the nearby sea.

With some misgivings we drew off on to the only dry patch of gravel on the site. We would consider the situation. It certainly looked as though, with another inch or two of rain, the whole area would again revert to Zuyder Zee.

Was there any point in staying? What we had hoped to find here could surely be found elsewhere. It was then that we heard, from the dyke-intersected quagmire of meadowland adjoining the caravan site, a sudden and glorious outpouring of wader cries. Sailing through the air towards us and calling as he came was a magnificent Black-tailed Godwit. He alighted fifty yards away and we watched him through the caravan window as he paced restlessly to and fro. He was a territorially-minded bird. His nest could not be far away. We scanned the sodden marshland. Half a dozen Godwits were stalking about there, and Lapwings, Redshanks and Snipe were all in evidence. But, best of all, there were Ruffs – Ruffs on a tilting-ground – a dozen birds sparring and prancing about in a gleam of late afternoon sunshine. By the greatest good fortune we had discovered a few acres of marsh which might well provide us with all the photographic opportunities we could hope for at this particular stage of our journey. To encounter Ruffs on a tilting-ground and Godwits in their breeding meadows – these were two of the primary objectives of our visit to the Netherlands. It was just possible that we could achieve both objectives within sight of the caravan on this particular site. Rain, hail or flood – we would stay here for the next two days.

The friendly owner of the caravan site soon discovered our interest in birds. With expressive pugilistic gestures he confirmed for us the presence of Ruffs in the near-by field – the only place in the region where they were to be found. He gave us to understand that although it was in a sense a 'protected' area, access was not forbidden. We were free to explore and to film and photograph to our heart's content. We needed no further invitation.

After a quick meal we donned rubber boots and set forth to investigate the possibilities. A score of birds rose to meet us as we crossed the marsh, and we were accompanied by yelping Godwits, yodelling Redshanks and chippering Snipe, and by Lapwings that dive-bombed us as we crossed their territories. We made for the Ruffs' tilting-ground to see what prospects it held for the erection of a hide. The nearer we approached the more waterlogged became the terrain. When we finally reached the spot where they had been displaying we found that it was entirely surrounded by quaking bog that was now, thanks to the rain of the past twenty-four hours, under several inches of water. Bird photography under these conditions might almost be classified as an aquatic sport. The camouflaged hide we had brought with us and which we proposed to erect was only a low, squatting affair some four feet high. Once installed within, it was necessary to adopt either a kneeling or a squatting posture. But whichever one chose for this particular operation – the western attitude for prayer or the eastern posture for contemplation – the plain fact was that the experience would be far more endurable if not performed in six or more inches of water. A possible alleviation of the situation came with the discovery of some ancient bundles of reeds lying beside a dyke some fifty yards away. Piled on top of each other and covered with a waterproof sheet these should ensure reasonably dry kneeling or seating within. Backwards and forwards we squelched, bearing our sodden bundles until sufficient were assembled for our purpose. The hide was then erected on top of the reed platform; some surplus reed bundles were draped round its sides, and all was in readiness for the morrow. As darkness fell we returned to the caravan. Everything now depended on the weather. Another night like last night and the tilting-ground would be totally submerged.

At 5 a.m. we were awakened by a tremendous tattoo of hail on the caravan roof. There followed half an hour of torrential rain and the situation appeared hopeless.

But as light strengthened and it became possible to peer with binoculars across the flooded marsh we could detect a flurry and scurry on the area where the hide was sited. In spite of the appalling weather the Ruffs were undismayed. Why should we lose heart? By half-past six the rain had stopped and blue sky was showing. By seven o'clock we were crossing the marsh and heading for the Ruffs' domain. Water, water everywhere – but the actual water level had not risen appreciably as yet. The Ruffs were displaying on their accustomed site and only dispersed with some reluctance at our approach. Within ten minutes of my installation within the hide the first Ruffs arrived. For a few moments they stood uncertainly, and then, when a female – a Reeve – came flying past, they lost all fear and began their fantastic display.

It was exactly as I remembered it from our first visit to Holland fifteen years ago when Jan Strijbos, our host, had installed us in a hide beside a reedy mere near Knollendam. There was the same flaring out of multi-coloured ruffs and lappets as they began sparring at one another, prancing up and down in a curiously stiff and formalized way. Some crouched forward with beaks rigidly downpointed; others flattened themselves on the grass in a trance-like state of immobility. But every few minutes the whole scene changed with a kaleidoscopic suddenness, and the arrival of a Reeve was always the prelude to a violent paroxysm of emotional fervour from the males. Apart from an occasional clapping of wings when two opposing birds mounted the air, the whole performance was conducted in a strange and unexpected silence. It was like watching an endless puppet show in which no purposeful action ever seemed to take place.

69

These extraordinary birds, arrayed like Elizabethan gallants with gorgeous ruffs and trappings, swash-buckling across their narrow stage and indulging in a frenzy of mock heroics, were all the time miming their parts and giving the impression that their mechanical motions were the actions not of sentient creatures but of automata.

And yet the pattern of this display and the stimulus of social encounter must play a vital part in the fulfilment of their breeding-cycle; otherwise it would not continue from dawn till dusk, week after week, until the nesting-season is far advanced. Close observation has shown that the Ruffs are not, in fact, battling for possession of the females – the Reeves.

It is the Reeves who make the choice of their respective partners. They walk about serenely among the posturing males, and their selection of partners indicates that it is by no means always the Ruff with the most handsome plumage or the most extravagant display who attracts a mate. Nowadays we tend to seek for an interpretation of bird behaviour in terms of territory, and of ceremonial threat and courtship display. It seems that in the Ruff we have an extreme example of a bird whose territory has shrunk to the smallest possible size – a square foot of trampled turf will suffice, providing this is immediately adjacent to similar territories of other contesting males. The pugilistic tendency in males, if directed savagely against its own kind, is inherently dangerous to the survival of a species. In the Ruff this tendency has almost completely been assimilated into ritual dance and posture, so that it becomes difficult to determine where one breaks off and another begins. Two birds fronting each other may suddenly rise in the air, breast to breast, with violently flapping wings, exactly like game-cocks. On alighting, one may rear up for a second encounter; the other has slipped into another phase of display, and is now seen crouching flat, with lappets flared out and quivering, or standing stiff and rigid, with bill downpointed and ruff outspread, flaunting its masculine adornments in mute appeal to any passing Reeve.

For an hour I played the part of an unseen Gulliver in this avian Lilliput. It was time to be relieved from my cramped quarters, but I was left with the feeling that to understand more fully the significance of all that I had seen would require far more time than this brief encounter would allow.

Meanwhile two more tilting-grounds had been discovered in adjacent fields, and a Marsh Harrier had been observed rising from a reed bed near at hand. It was while going off in search of these that a sitting Black-tailed Godwit was flushed from her nest which contained four lovely eggs deep in a tussock of grass embowered with marsh marigolds and cuckoo flowers. An attempt was made the following morning to accustom her to a hide, but she was apprehensive and we did not press the point. Meanwhile there were distant shots to be taken of the other Ruffs' tilting-grounds, another Godwit's nest to be tracked down, and a very small Rail, no larger than a Starling, that scuttled rat-like from one reed bed to another, to be identified. It was almost certainly a Little Crake, but would not show itself a second time.

We enjoyed our two days in the 'vaterland' – two days of splashing around in waterproofs and wellingtons – but we felt now that we were due for a change of scene. Texel was calling, so we made for Den Helder where the island is clearly visible across the sound. We were sorely tempted to make an immediate crossing. There is a magic about Texel that is difficult to resist. But we withstood the temptation for at Zwannenwater, on the north-west tip of the Dutch coast, is a famous Spoonbill breeding reserve. There is, in fact, a similar Spoonbill reserve on Texel, but we felt we should be failing in our duty if we did not pay our respects to both.

7

Texel – Island of Birds

ZWANNENWATER reserve is a good example of conservation as practised in the Netherlands. Visitors to the reserve must first obtain a permit at the Warden's house. They are not taken on a closely conducted tour but are permitted to wander unaccompanied, provided they keep to 'excursie pads' – well-defined footpaths from which it is not permitted to stray in search of birds and flowers.

The Spoonbill breeding-area is, understandably, not accessible to visitors, but occasional birds can be seen flying overhead – beautiful, graceful, snow-white creatures particularly if seen against the blue of the sky. The footpath meanders past reed beds alive with Sedge and Reed Warblers and loud with their song. It traverses an area of duneland from the top of which one can look down on Herons' nests in tall bushes a short distance away. The young ones in the nests were well advanced at this time of year, and we spent an interesting hour filming the parents returning with food. Zwannenwater with its trodden paths and carefully signposted routes provides the interested visitor with a very pleasant 'Nature Trail'. There is inevitably a feeling of being controlled and directed – very necessarily so, for how else can you organize access to a popular mainland reserve? But we were pining for open spaces where we could wander without restriction. And Texel was beckoning, a short hour's voyage away.

Texel is the first of that chain of lovely bird islands along the North Sea coast of the Netherlands. It is some fifteen miles long and five miles wide. It is the oldest island in the Netherlands, and its core is a glacial deposit laid down in Pleistocene times. Around this solid centre the rest of the island has been formed by polder reclamation, and by the gradual building up of vast accumulations of sand on the western dunes.

Texel has featured in the history of the Netherlands very many times. Admiral Van Tromp, scourge of the British Fleet, met his death in July, 1653, in a day-long encounter against Blake, Dean and Monk, in the off-shore waters of Texel. In 1794, Pichegron, a daring and able French general, turned the hard winter to good account by taking his cavalry on to the ice and capturing the Dutch fleet as it lay ice-bound between Texel and Den Helder. British troops occupied Texel during the last year of that century, and in that same year the treasure ship *La Lutine* was wrecked off the neighbouring island of Vlieland. Her ship's bell has become famous at Lloyds, who also possess a chair and table made from her rudder. In 1857 a Dutch salvage company recovered nearly £100,000 from the wreck, but more than ten times that amount still stays strewn among the North Sea tides.

In 1940, Texel, in German hands, became a northern bastion of the Atlantic Wall. It was a strategic point in the defence system and was furnished with a strong coast battery. A fighter airfield was established in the middle of the island. The large infantry garrison on Texel included 750 Russian prisoners-of-war pressed into the German army. About a month before V.E. Day the Russians rose in the night and slew the entire German garrison except the remote shore batteries behind their mine-fields. One German officer escaped to the main-land. The following day he returned with over a thousand reinforcements and some tanks. A month of epic battle followed. The Russians, heavily outnumbered, were shelled not only from the Texel batteries but from the mainland as well. V.E. Day came just in time to save them. The Germans had suffered 2,000 casualties; the Russians 500. The 250 survivors were returned to a Russian camp and given full credit for the gallant part they played in this uprising against their German masters.

From Den Helder we took a late evening ferry to Texel. We disembarked in failing light, but we were not unduly concerned at the lateness of the hour. We were on familiar ground: we had been here before. Fifteen years had passed, but it was just as we remembered it – the turf walls marking field boundaries in the south of the island, and Oyster-catchers – Texel's Sea Pies – trotting off the road verges at our approach.

The island is so conveniently small that if you have some means of transport it matters not where you make your base. We decided to make for a caravan site in the far north, near the dunes on the outskirts of Cocksdorp, and not far from the lighthouse. Half an hour later we were installed for the night. Away to the north-west the Cocksdorp lighthouse winked away merrily in the velvet dark. Restless Oyster-catchers yickered and piped, and, from time to time, strange unidentified calls rained down from the quiet skies as a rush of wings told of migration in progress. Texel, Island of Birds, was weaving its spell.

But towards dawn rain set in, and continued until mid-morning – and with the rain came a growing feeling of frustration. Here we were on this lovely island surrounded by its wildlife and confined to the caravan for fear of getting wet. We had spare clothes: now was the time to use them. The decision taken, the sky immediately grew lighter. The rain moderated to a fine drizzle, and by the time we were setting forth the sun was almost through.

We made at once for the middle of the island – for the Walenburg polder with its intersecting roads, its windpumps and its flooded meadows. This is one of the oldest and most delightful of the reserves on Texel. It is a simple demonstration of what can happen when an area of partially-drained polder is left in its natural state to attract the birds that favour these conditions, and having attracted them is then sealed off as a protected area where they can breed undisturbed.

There was one difference that we noted in the Walenburg that we saw today compared with the Walenburg of fifteen years before. There was more water lying around. Was this the accidental result of unusually heavy rainfall in recent days – or was it intentional? We were later to learn that this was the result of deliberate policy. It had been done in the hope of attracting Ruffs and Reeves back to the reserve, and it had succeeded. Thirty or forty years ago Walenburg was famous for its

Ruffs and Reeves. Bird-lovers came from far and near to enjoy the unusual spectacle of Ruffs gathering for their pugilistic display on the rough roads that crossed the polder. Improvements in drainage methods in mid-Texel, however, resulted in the whole area gradually drying out. Year by year the number of Ruffs diminished, and the Walenburg was steadily losing one of its principal assets. On our previous visit we had not seen any Ruffs on this reserve. An enlightened policy of spring-time flooding was then suggested, and was experimentally carried out. The Ruffs made an immediate and spectacular return. We were acquainted with these facts when we met the Warden later in the day. The first intimation that we now had of anything unusual was a road sign warning motorists to beware of 'vogels'. We scanned the road ahead, and there on the road verge just off the tarmac were half a dozen birds rushing belligerently to and fro. The Walenburg Ruffs were back, and, in their choice of battle-ground were behaving absolutely true to form. They were on the same type of roadside tilting ground that their forebears had favoured at the turn of the century. Quietly we slid the car nearer. When we were eight yards away we halted. Carefully a window was opened to allow the camera lens to peep out. The click of the shutter and the whirr of the ciné motor were completely disregarded. The Ruffs refused to be distracted, each bird clinging tenaciously to its individual stand, a square foot of roadside grass on which it crouched and postured. Even a passing motor-cycle failed to dislodge them although it passed within feet of where they were standing.

Meanwhile other sights and sounds were tempting us

to continue our exploratory journey along the polder road. The marsh was alive with waders and the air full of their music. Above the piping of Oyster-catchers could be heard the wild spring cries of Peewit and Redshank, Avocet and Godwit, each uttering its own distinctive call – its own name in the Dutch language – Kievit and Tureluur, Kluit and Grutto.

It was hatching time for Godwit families – the Black-tailed Godwit is a month earlier than the northern-nesting 'Bar-tail'. Downy young were staggering about in the meadow grass and occasionally straying near to the roadside ditches. Their agitated parents came yelping overhead, dive-bombing us as we left the car, or alighting on fence-posts. Emboldened by parental anxiety and looking splendidly Texelian against that background of flooded polder, they allowed us to approach to within reasonable photographic range.

Commonest and most obvious of all the polder birds were the nesting Oyster-catchers. Each time we halted we could count three or four birds sitting on nests out on the moist meadows. One pair, however, had chosen a drier situation. As we brought the car to rest beside a pile of gravel on the roadside, we were fortunate to catch a quick glimpse of a black head and orange bill disappearing from view as an Oyster-catcher slipped away from her nest on top of the gravel heap.

It was time to tear ourselves away. We had an appointment to keep at De Koog, and permits to obtain for visits to De Muij, the Texel Spoonbill reserve on the western shore, and for De Geul, a dune sanctuary in the south-west.

We had an interesting talk with the Assistant Warden

for these reserves in his office at De Koog. He spoke of a sad decline in the number of nesting Spoonbills at De Muij. Last year there were seventy to eighty pairs: this year only half that number. Dead Spoonbills had been found in various parts of the island at the end of the breeding season last year. Their bodies contained dieldrin, one of the insecticide poisons. The bulb growers may be to blame. Bulbs are sterilized in tanks of insecticide fluid. Some growers carelessly dump the used fluid in the nearest ditch, and Spoonbills frequent ditches when questing with those curious spatulate bills of theirs for water snails, beetles and other aquatic delicacies.

We obtained our permits to join 'excursie' parties that would be visiting De Muij and De Geul the following day, and we then returned across the Walenburg to reconnoitre the sea wall on the east coast just north of Oost. We had recollections from our previous visit to Texel of watching Brent Geese flighting from the flooded saltings and coming in to alight on green meadows beside a lake overlooked by a most impressive windmill.

It was exactly as we remembered it. As we climbed the great soil bank that forms the sea wall a long line of eighty geese could be seen approaching. They passed almost overhead before planing down to alight on the grass beside the mill. We spent an hour watching the geese and noting other birds in the vicinity – three hundred Bar-tailed Godwits resting in a dense pack on ploughed land, half a dozen Eiders swimming out at sea with some Tufted Ducks and Mergansers, and seven Avocets in the shallow lagoon that flanked the sea wall.

Where next? We had sampled the Walenburg: we

had visited De Koog: we had re-acquainted ourselves with the goose mill. Why not the western dunes? The delightful thing about Texel is its size. It is not too small to be cramped nor is it too broken up to lose the feeling of space. It is large enough to satisfy whilst retaining its sense of homeliness and peace. By car you can cross from its eastern to its western coast in about fifteen minutes, but it took us a full hour. At every turning of the road there was something to halt us – a Mallard leading a dozen newly-hatched ducklings across the road and into the shelter of a reedy ditch; a Spotted Redshank in splendid dusky plumage pausing on migration for a quick meal in the flooded meadows; a pair of Spoonbills dibbling in a shallow pool.

It was late afternoon when we finally climbed the dunes and looked out upon the North Sea. Much of the dune area on the western coast is reserved for wildlife and access is limited, but we were in a free area which we could explore without being guilty of trespass.

We noticed at once the evidence of a nation-wide concern for strengthening the sea defences. Wherever a bare patch of sand had appeared as a result of wind erosion new tufts of marram grass had been planted. In places where driven sand was on the move, branches of pine from a nearby plantation belt were strewn about to arrest the flow. It is difficult to convey a true impression of the size and extent of the Texel dunes to anyone who has not seen them. A full half-mile in depth, they extend for the whole fifteen miles of the western coastline, maintaining a steady height of fifty to a hundred feet. This vast accumulation of sand has, of course, been deliberately encouraged for centuries by the

The Étang de Vaccares in the Camargue,
with Flamingoes in the distance.

1

A change-over of duties at a Stork's
nest.   Le Zwin, Belgium.

Ruffs and Reeves at a 'tilting-ground'
near Ouitdam, Holland.

2

Avocet questing for food in choppy
water.   Oost, Texel.

planting of sea buckthorn and creeping willow in the hollows, and marram grass on the hills. It is a wild and solitary region where bird life is not plentiful. Herring Gulls, cliff-nesters in Britain, breed in colonies on the less frequented, hill-top areas. Hundreds of Jackdaws nest colonially in rabbit burrows close by. We were hoping to find Kentish Plovers on the shoreline, but found only Oyster-catchers nesting there. On our return journey we passed through one of the conifer belts planted in the lee of the dunes, and surprised a Long-eared Owl from its daytime roost, but by now we were too tired and hungry to stay for a fuller investigation. We had been on the move for ten hours on haversack rations. It was time we returned for a proper meal.

The two 'excursies' arranged for the following day were due to take place at 10 a.m. and 2 p.m. We arrived at De Muij in very good time, determined not to start off on the wrong foot. We had slight misgivings about conducted tours. Bird-watching is essentially a solitary pastime. It does not lend itself to mass-meandering. There would also be the difficulty of communication. Our knowledge of the Dutch language was virtually non-existent, and we could hardly expect our guide to converse in our language. In fact, we were later to find that on both morning and afternoon tours of the reserves our guides conversed in very good English. This was very fortunate for on both occasions the excursion parties included American tourists who were as lin-guistically handicapped as we were.

From the Warden's hut we approached the dunes along a footpath through gently rising meadowland where Oyster-catchers were nesting. When we first sighted the Spoonbill colony it appeared so distant that any hopes of photography even at extreme range were dashed. They were nesting in company with Herons in reeds and low bushes on an island far out in a vast lake set in the heart of the dunes. There was a constant coming and going of birds, but even at a range of three or four hundred yards surprisingly good views were obtained through binoculars. It was a great pleasure and privilege to be watching one of Europe's largest and rarest breeding birds conducting its domestic affairs securely under the vigilant eye of the Dutch conservation authorities.

After we had had our fill of Spoonbills we moved along the 'excursie pad' and were shown a good selection of nests that lay within easy reach of the pathway – a grass hollow where four young Curlews were just hatching and drying off – a Shoveler's nest that contained, as well as its own full clutch, three Pheasant's eggs, the result of random laying. We were shown a Redshank crouching motionless in the heart of a grass tussock, a Teal's nest in a clump of sedge, and nests of Godwits and Lapwings on a stretch of open marsh. All in all we found we had spent a thoroughly enjoyable two hours in very congenial company.

To be in readiness for the afternoon's tour of the De Geul reserve we travelled south and had our picnic lunch beside a muddy tidal creek that bears the expressive name of Mokbaai. Hundreds of waders were searching for food on the mud flats, and scores of Shelducks were dibbling in the ooze. But what immediately attracted our attention was a snow-white Oyster-catcher – a pure albino – that was trotting about along the edge of the creek and engaging in 'piping parties' with other Oyster-catchers there. It was clearly seeking a mate – and equally clearly having difficulties in overcoming its plumage disability. Again and again it approached other small groups of Oyster-catchers but they always, disappointingly, moved away. The Warden at De Geul told us later that it had been hanging about this muddy creek for the past three years without achieving breeding success.

After lunch we assembled at the Warden's hut. It looked as though it would be quite a small party for the afternoon's outing, but just as we were setting forth for the reserve a coach drew up and out of it poured a score of weather-beaten, ruddy-faced farmers all wearing rubber boots and waterproofs. They were Frieslanders out on a Saturday spree and – as we were shortly to discover – all eager for an opportunity of indulging in their own particular sport. The De Geul reserve is a mixture of marsh and dune. To reach the duneland you must first traverse an area of squelching bog. The moment we set foot on this terrain a Lapwing took to the air and began its plaintive mewing. Without a word spoken the Frieslanders immediately charged into the bog, and, once there, proceeded to pace eagerly to and fro with eyes riveted to the ground. The Warden had meanwhile moved a little to one side and was waiting for developments with an amused smile on his face. We went to join him and asked what was happening. He explained that the finding of Lapwings' nests is a local sporting activity pursued with enormous fervour by the people of Friesland, and they are justly famed for their skill and keen eyesight. Throughout Holland the farming of

Lapwings' eggs takes place every year until mid-April, after which the bird comes under the most rigid protection. There is intense rivalry in country districts to find the earliest clutches. The first eggs to be found are always sent to the Queen, and it is a great honour to be their discoverer. Very few Lapwings in Holland hatch out their first clutches, but in practice this may well work out to the bird's advantage. Second clutches are laid when harrowing is finished, when there is better protective cover for the hatching chicks, and when the weather is more favourable.

While this explanation was being made it became more and more obvious that the enthusiasm of the Frieslanders was flagging. Reluctantly they gave up their fruitless search and came back to the waiting Warden. This was the moment he had been waiting for. Now for the 'coup de grâce'. 'The nest you are looking for,' he said, 'is here.' And there it was in the angle formed by his out-turned feet. There were roars of laughter . . . lots of good humour . . . endless chaff and banter. The Frieslanders were delighted at being so splendidly discomfited. This had made their day.

We now set off for a serious exploration of the reserve. Almost immediately a great golden-eyed owl floated up from a tussock of reeds. We expected a nest but found only a roosting platform, but the Warden said that this pair of Short-eared Owls had a nest deep in the marsh but were not to be disturbed. Close by the path were nests of Mallard, Shoveler and Teal, and we were shown a Pheasant's nest containing a duck egg – a curious reversal of what we had seen a few hours earlier at De Muij.

We climbed the dunes and visited a colony of Jackdaws. Many of the rabbit holes normally occupied on these high dunes had been provided with nesting-boxes sunk into the entrance holes so that inspection of the occupants could take place. Several were opened up for our interest. They contained eggs or half-grown young, and one or two parents crouched low over their offspring and refused to leave. Jackdaws are becoming almost too numerous on Texel, so when the young in the boxes are ready to leave they are removed and sent away to be released in parts of Holland where they have a scarcity value and are greatly welcomed.

Rain marred the final stages of our excursion, but before it was over we had an opportunity of watching the Frieslanders demonstrate their skill. While crossing a stretch of marshy meadowland two Lapwings' nests and a Redshank's were found in an incredibly short space of time. Honour thus retrieved, the Frieslanders departed in their coach for pastures new, while we set forth across the island for De Waal. We wanted to meet the Warden of the Walenburg, Mr. Boot, whose father and grandfather had managed the reserve before him.

A keen, energetic young fellow, he had under his surveillance not only the Walenburg polder but also the goose mill near Oost, and the salt marsh behind the sea wall – the famous Schorren.

On our previous visit to Texel we had lain on the bank overlooking the Schorren and watched Bar-tailed Godwits in their thousands swirling over the green marsh as the tide came in. Ever since that day it had been an ambition of ours to revisit the Schorren, learn its geography, and discover a site for a hide that would command a view of some muddy creek up which, driven by the oncoming tide, the Godwits would come. An hour or two in such a hide could be most rewarding.

We explained all this to the Warden who listened sympathetically, but who told us that without a specific permit from the organization controlling the reserve such a thing was impossible. As Warden he had his strict instructions to carry out, and these included the refusal of permission to erect hides in the reserve. For the Godwits he recommended an unrestricted area of coast near Cocksdorp in the north. Often, when the Schorren was flooded at high tide, the Godwits massed there, and we could put up a hide without anyone objecting. He would, however, be delighted to conduct us to a permanent hide sited by the edge of the lake near the mill from which we might get good views of Brent Geese flighting in and grazing on the meadow grass. We accepted his offer and made arrangements to be at the mill the following morning.

We returned to the caravan for a late tea, and afterwards went to reconnoitre the coast north of the Schorren. We could see that it was an area full of promise, but first it would be necessary to find out exactly where the birds assembled after high tide. Another intriguing possibility also presented itself. From a shell-beach just above the high-tide line came a subdued and plaintive piping. Two Kentish Plovers were trotting anxiously to and fro. Almost certainly they had a nest.

During the night the wind veered to the west and strengthened. By dawn a full gale was blowing accompanied by heavy rain. Our caravan shuddered and staggered, and the noise was deafening. There seemed little prospect of an improvement in weather conditions and we were uncertain what to do for we had arranged our meeting at the mill at 10 a.m. Would the Warden be there under these conditions? Yes, we decided, he probably would – he looked that sort of fellow, and it would not do to let him down. So after a hasty breakfast we struggled into waterproof clothing and set forth with the wind blowing great guns but the rain now lessening.

By the time we reached the sea wall the sky was clearing, and apart from the incessant wind there was the promise of a very pleasant day. Sure enough the Warden was there to greet us. He installed us in one of the hides by the pool side. During the night the other had been uprooted by the wind and bowled clean over into the lake. He wished us good luck, expressed the hope that our hide would not share the same fate in the next hour or so, and departed.

For two hours we crouched in that draughty hide with the wind howling round us. Some geese flew in but alighted two hundred yards away. Our best shots were of Avocets feeding in shallow water near the hide. Under normal conditions they would have heard the whirr of the ciné motor and been suspicious, but the wind was making such a racket that this additional sound went unobserved. A pair of Oyster-catchers were building a nest some thirty yards away, and a pair of Blue-headed Wagtails came dancing daintily on the greensward a few paces from our hiding place.

On being released from our draughty quarters we made for the unrestricted coastal strip at Cocksdorp to see it under high tide conditions. A conglomeration of stones some way out on the mud flats suggested a possible site for a hide. We laboured for a quarter of an hour piling up the stones to form a wall behind which we could crouch – glancing apprehensively shorewards the while and wondering what dire punishment could be inflicted by Dutch law on the agents of a foreign power found tampering with the coastal defences of the Netherlands. Although it was nearing high-tide few waders were on the move, so we withdrew to the shell-beach to look for the Kentish Plovers. They were there again and we took turns to lie in concealment in the hope of seeing one or other of the birds back to the nesting-scrape. Our concentration on the Kentish Plovers, however, evaporated completely when, on the ebb-tide, a vast host of Godwits came streaming over and began settling, not in front of our stone wall but a hundred yards or more to the east where some lines of brushwood projected out to sea. This would be a possible screen behind which hides could be erected on the morrow. The Godwits made a tremendous sight, their russet breasts glowing in the evening sun. Several thousand of them had now assembled in a hundred-yard-long line along the edge of the receding tide. Photographically there were immense opportunities, but the time factor was all-important. Had they arrived ten minutes later the tide would have receded another fifty yards and they would have been out of photographic range.

We had another windy night with grey skies and fast-scudding clouds at dawn, so we turned over in our bunks and were alarmed, on waking a second time, to find the sun well up and a lot of preparations to be made before we headed for the northern shore. At last we were ready, but we lacked a supply of safety pins. On a windy day these are vitally necessary for preventing flapping from the cloth of the hide. No doubt the village store in Cocksdorp would oblige. The good lady in the shop could not speak English, but in anticipation of difficulties in this direction I had furnished myself with a small sample of the required article. I brandished my little safety-pin and indicated that I wanted many of them, giant-size. An understanding smile spread over her face. She rummaged in a drawer and produced exactly what was required – two cards of extra large pins, complete with a picture of Stork with baby in nappy suspended from its bill. Beaming with solicitude she handed me the pins, and sought to convey in fluent Dutch what could only have been her warmest congratulations on my recent paternity. I bowed my acknowledgment, and, clutching the nappy pins, retired forthwith in some confusion.

When we reached the mud flats the tide was coming in but there was still ample time for preparations. After quite a struggle in the strong wind we pegged down our hides behind the line of brushwood, rendered them more or less flap-proof with a liberal use of those excellent nappy pins, and retired within. A few Shelducks were swimming in the lagoon away to our right. A score of Oyster-catchers were hanging about the shore line, but of other waders there was no sign – nor did we expect them for an hour or two yet. With the flooding of the Schorren marshes the Godwits would first flight inland to rest on ploughland behind the sea wall. It was on the ebb-tide that we pinned our hopes of interviewing them here.

The first birds to provide us with interest were Eiders — a score of them, ducks and drakes, swimming out at sea but steadily nearing the shore. Eventually they effected a landing, but a hundred yards away. Eiders are recent colonists here. It seems that Vlieland and other islands up the North Sea coast are now sending to Texel their surplus. Elsewhere in the Netherlands the status of the Eider is improving year by year.

A few Turnstones arrived and pottered about along the tide-line. If ever we reached the Arctic Sea this was a bird whose nest we hoped to find. A pair of Shelducks came very close — some ten to fifteen yards away — and walked past the hides a trifle suspiciously.

Gradually the water crept closer: at high tide it was just three paces from our hides, and then began the slow ebb. Time passed. A muddy margin was now showing. Conditions would soon be ideal. The minutes dragged by — but where were the Godwits? Yesterday at this stage of the tide they were here in their thousands. The light had never been good: now it was worsening. As the minutes slipped by, the edge of the tide on which the cameras were trained retreated steadily. It was obvious that the Godwits had let us down. And then, just as we were considering giving up, the air was suddenly filled with the rush of wings. In poured the Godwits, great swirling masses of them, and down they came into the shallow water — a superb spectacle, but, alas, by now at extreme photographic range. A long burst of ciné was whirred off at them as they came in to alight. The motor was rewound, and, as another flock came streaming in, the lens was opened to full aperture and the speed pushed up to 64 frames a second, and film blazed away for as long as the motor held out. It was a haphazard affair and the outcome appeared most uncertain. What a happy surprise to find, a fortnight later when film came back from processing during our stay in Denmark, that these two sequences were technically as good as any that had been taken on the journey so far.

For a bird-watcher the spectacle of massed wader flight has a quality all of its own. The record obtained during the last few minutes of our long vigil on Texel's northern shore-line more than repaid us for the rigours of the day. The Godwits were now moving further and further away as the tide went down. We were stiff and cold after seven hours of crouching in our hides. Fingers were numb, and it took a full ten minutes to dismantle our apparatus and stow it away. Then followed a laboured return across the mud flats to the shore and the waiting car. Inside, we gasped with relief at escaping from the wind – and looked at our watches. It was after seven. It had been a long day.

We slept late the following morning for we had already decided that this was to be a day of relaxation. In the morning we revisited the Oost mill to see if there were any geese about, and were fortunate to have a skein fly over. We crossed the Walenburg polder once again and photographed a Black-tailed Godwit yelling at us from a gate post. We returned to the shell-beach at Cocksdorp, and in a highly successful five minutes found a White Wagtail nesting in the dunes, and the Kentish Plover's nest we had searched for in vain on two previous occasions. The nesting-scrape contained two eggs only, and it seemed premature to attempt photography. We returned to base to find a party of our own countrymen pitching tents nearby. They, too, were on a bird-watching holiday, and we passed a pleasant hour with them later in the evening. One had been to the Arctic Sea the previous summer, and he fired our enthusiasm for the far north with a description of the birds he had seen in Varanger Fjord. He drew us a map which was to prove invaluable later on.

The next day began disastrously. We were on the point of departure. The Bedford responded as usual to the first touch of the self-starter. We were feeling a little self-satisfied about this, for our neighbours were experiencing some difficulty in getting their car to start after a night out in heavy dew. But as I climbed into the front seat and sat down there was a colossal 'wumph', followed by the crackle of disintegrating vulcanite and the sound of escaping fluid. The car engine had died on the instant, and, hissing and gurgling on the grass under the car, lay the shattered remains of our 12-volt accumulator. Some electrical short must have caused the explosion, and until we could get mechanical help and a new accumulator we were completely immobilized. The chances of getting either on this remote island seemed slender indeed. We found a workman doing repairs on a near-by chalet and he came over to see for himself. He shook his head at the sorry sight but indicated to us that he would telephone for help. Within a quarter of an hour a van had arrived. A young mechanic stepped out. Briskly and efficiently he inspected the damage, pointed to a frayed lead that had caused an electrical short with the car chassis, produced from the van a new battery of the right size, fitted it, re-insulated the leads, tested, presented his bill, was paid, shook hands and departed.

All in all the disaster cost us an hour's delay and the price of a new battery. We got off very lightly.

One result of the mishap, however, was that we were practically cleaned out of Dutch guilders, and so a visit to the nearest Bank at Den Burg to cash Traveller's Cheques was imperative.

When we had transacted our business in this attractive little Texel town we returned to the northern shore to photograph the Kentish Plover. It proved to be a reasonably easy subject, and we had time in addition to try for some stalking shots of a great Oyster-catcher assembly at the edge of the tide.

They made a brave sight, standing there in shallow water, with the afternoon sun slanting low across the mud flats and giving an added brilliance to the contrasting black and white of their plumage – five hundred Oyster-catchers in their pied livery, with orange bills and pink legs glowing in the sunshine – a sight to remember. And the air was filled with their cries – pipings and kleepings and yickerings – a splendid confusion of tumultuous sound. The tape-recorder was much in evidence during that hour with the Oyster-catchers and some fine recordings were made.

The tape-recorder was to come into use again later that evening when we went for a walk in the duneland in the gathering dusk. For half a mile or more the pathway was flanked on either side by thickets of bramble, sea-buckthorn and creeping willow. It was almost dark and most birds had retired for the night, but from one of these thickets came the persistent 'reeling' song of a Grasshopper Warbler.

More than once in the past I had crept up to within

close viewing distance of a singing Grasshopper Warbler in some neglected, unfrequented spot where heath and marsh adjoined. I knew from experience that the bird becomes so wholly absorbed at such a time, its whole body vibrating and its head, with open bill, turning from side to side, that it is possible with caution to approach to within a yard or two.

With the microphone pointed forward and the tape-recorder switched on, I began my stealthy approach. As long as the bird continued singing I kept up my cautious, step by step, advance. The moment it stopped to regain breath I froze in my tracks. In this way I finally crept up to within three yards of the hidden bird. At this close range the high, metallic, percussive notes smote almost painfully on the ear drums. At a distance the Grass-hopper Warbler's song has been aptly likened to the sound of line running off an angler's reel. At close quarters it resembled a high-pitched pneumatic drill. In the darkness I had to judge the level of sound by guess-work. To be on the safe side I made a whole series of recordings on widely differing settings. But it was advisable to have a replay as soon as possible to make sure that all was well. Silently I withdrew and retraced my steps until I was about fifty yards away from the singing bird. The tape was wound back and the record-ing tested. The first, distant approach shots were quite good: the near ones were terrific.

It was then, as I knelt on the grass in the half-dark listening to 'reeling' notes as they came throbbing from the tape-recorder, that a remarkable thing happened. There was a sudden, high-pitched 'chitter...chitter' noise just behind me as a small aggressive bird, its wings rasping and rustling defiantly, came fluttering on to my shoulder. From there it scuttled, mouse-like, down my chest towards the tape-recorder. It stayed but a moment, and then whizzed away with harsh scolding notes into the bushes near at hand. I switched off the tape-recorder and listened. With one or two snatches of angry song from intermediate stations, the outraged bird made its way back to its original thicket and was soon 'reeling' away as though nothing had happened. It was a vivid demonstration of the part played by song in the definition of territory in a small bird's world. That powerful, sustained song of the Grasshopper Warbler was both an assertion and a challenge. A rival would know what to expect. I had unwittingly provided that rival, and had been privileged to witness his attempted eviction.

On the way back we tried out the same technique on another Grasshopper Warbler singing equally lustily in some low bushes nearer our base. The moon had risen and it was appreciably lighter now, so we sat down in the shadow of a bramble thicket some fifty yards from the singing bird. We let him get nicely launched into a sustained burst of song and then switched on. Instantly his own song stopped. There was a pause of a second or two – just long enough for an outraged little bird to fly fifty yards into the attack – and then, suddenly, the air was full of fluttering wings and harsh little jarring cries as he darted here and there in search of his rival. It was all over in fifteen seconds, but for half of that time, angry and perplexed, he was hopping about on my brother's knee. As with the first Grasshopper Warbler this little bird did not loiter once a visible rival was not to be found. He hastened back to his original tangle of scrub and recommenced his singing there without further ado. Nor could any further playing over of the recording tempt him back again. We found later in our journey that the Bluethroat in Lapland reacted to its own recorded song in exactly the same spirit of prompt aggression.

It would seem that in the tape-recorder the serious student of bird behaviour has now a new and valuable instrument for conducting experiments in this field. In the course of his experiments he should also have lots of fun!

Bar-tailed Godwits alighting on
mud-flats near Cocksdorp, Texel.

Black-tailed Godwit standing guard.
East Flevoland, Holland.

Young Long-eared Owl reared in a
nestbox on East Flevoland polder.

4

One of many Black-headed Gull colonies
in the Vejlerne Reserve, Jutland.

8

East Flevoland – A new Polder emerges from the Sea

IN OUR travel schedule we had allowed for a week on Texel, and the week was now over. For six days the wind had blown without ceasing, but now, on the seventh, it dropped completely. We crossed over to the mainland on a calm sea, and it was really warm at last. For the first time since entering Holland we could cast off our thick jerseys. In leisurely fashion we crossed the longest dyke in the world – the Ijsselmeer dam – that twenty-mile ramp of stones and earth which, in cutting the Zuyder Zee in two, had created the Ijsselmeer, a vast inland lake now in process of reclamation.

When the five new polders have eventually been drained, the Netherlands will have increased its land area by 550,000 acres.

The dam was started in 1927 and took five years to build. The first polder, Wieringermeer, was being reclaimed even as the dam went creeping across the Zuyder Zee and it was drained by the mid-thirties. The North-east polder of 120,000 acres was next enclosed between 1937 and 1942. Over 30,000 people now live there on smiling farmlands which, thirty years ago, were on the bed of the sea. East Flevoland is the most recent polder to be reclaimed. Its 133,000 acres were wrested from the Ijsselmeer between 1950 and 1957. Two more great areas of similar size are due for reclamation in the next few years. When the task is completed the area of arable land in the Netherlands will have been increased by ten per cent. The cost of this reclamation programme – about £500 per acre – would hardly be justified were it not known that large areas of the floor of the Zuyder Zee are covered with potentially fertile silt.

The emergence from the sea-bed of a vast area of potential farmland has exciting possibilities, not only for those who hope to till the soil, but also for the plant and animal communities that, given half a chance, will quickly exploit virgin territory and use it to their advantage.

An early stage in reclamation is the planting of reeds in the polder bed as the water level drops once pumping has become effective. This can only be successful when salinity has decreased sufficiently for land plants to gain a foothold. At the next stage, when the reed beds dry out and the first green flush of herbage spreads over the land, the invaders move in. In East Flevoland it was voles – voles that bred and multiplied in an astonishing way. In six years the vole population had grown to an estimated total of twenty millions.

How do you cope with twenty million voles? In many countries this would have been the signal for a wholesale campaign of extermination by poison. By scattering tons of poisoned bait all over the area by plane or helicopter a measure of control could no doubt have been gained. But such a policy would also have meant a wholesale contamination of the environment. And what about the other creatures living there? The quickest answer is not

necessarily the best. Already the reed beds were attracting the predators of voles. A hundred and fifty pairs of
Marsh Harriers had moved in. Why not a massive
campaign to encourage other natural predators of voles
by providing them with nesting accommodation? Kestrels and owls were needed – hundreds and hundreds of
them. A nesting-box project – unique in the history of
conservation – was launched. In the reed beds, in the
fenlands, in the newly-planted woodlands, hundreds of
roomy wooden boxes with half-open fronts were erected
on stout poles. They were about eight feet above ground
level, high enough to be out of the reach of jumping
dogs and foxes. In a short time seventy pairs of Kestrels
had moved in and families were being reared, and then
the Long-eared Owls followed suit. Short-eared Owls
which nest on the ground were already multiplying in
the reed beds. But Long-eared Owls require an elevated
site, and the Kestrel boxes proved entirely suitable to
their needs. Thus, in a comparatively short time, control
over the vole population had been established, and this
exercise in applied ecology can well serve as an object-
lesson to the rest of the world.

We had heard something of this nesting-box project
in East Flevoland, and we were eager to visit the area
so that we could see the scheme in action. We took the
coast road south along the former Zuyder Zee, through
a Dutch countryside much older in character than anything else we had so far encountered. Old thatched
farmsteads on high mounds now commanded a view
over the surrounding levels, and picturesque windmills,
brightly painted, gave a very distinctive Dutch atmosphere to the scene. The sun was setting as we neared

the town of Elburg on the outskirts of which we hoped to stay the night. A Long-eared Owl perching on a roadside tree stared down at us as we passed beneath. We halted the car some distance away and made a circuitous approach. The owl stood his ground and we had the satisfaction of photographing this noble bird at reasonably close range as it stared down at us from its lofty perch, its ear-tufts standing out in splendid silhouette against the sunset sky.

The air was warm and the atmosphere clear as we crossed over the bridge into the new polder, but no sooner had we entered East Flevoland than we became aware of a curious shifting haze that blurred the horizon. Wherever we looked there were phantom hosts swirling up and down. Millions and millions of gnats were making smoke-clouds over Flevoland. We were experiencing another population explosion – this time in the insect world.

We camped at the edge of the Ijsselmeer. The gnats were a nuisance but no more. At least they did not bite.

After a warm and windless night they were even more in evidence the following morning, but as we left the camp-site and entered the newly-planted timber belt in the north-eastern corner of the polder we left them behind. It was here that we hoped to see our first Kestrel boxes. We had no official permit to visit the area but trusted that any forester we might meet could be persuaded that our intentions were wholly honourable. In fact we did not meet a soul, but drove the Bedford gently and carefully up and down the woodland rides, stopping from time to time to inspect a nesting-box sited near the path. Of the six boxes we investigated one had young

Kestrels a few days' old, two had full clutches of Kestrel eggs, and one contained a young Long-eared Owl who glared balefully at us, clicked his beak, and generally conveyed a strong impression that our presence was far from welcome.

After the pleasant Owl and Kestrel interlude we decided to follow the road on the high enclosing dyke, and do a complete circuit of the polder – a journey of some forty to fifty miles with the Ijsselmeer always on our right and the new polder in its various stages of reclamation on our left.

To reach the dyke road we had to cross a barren region of dry sea-bed where farming operations had scarcely begun. It was a curious relic of the former sea floor, liberally sprinkled with sea shells and supporting a very sparse vegetation of samphire and sedge. We stopped again and again to scan this barren landscape. We were hoping for a glimpse of Holland's most remarkable breeding-birds – the Dotterels of Flevoland. If, a few decades ago, anyone had suggested the possibility of Dotterels becoming established as breeding-birds on the dried-out bed of the Zuyder Zee, the idea would have been greeted with incredulity if not with scorn. Elsewhere in Europe the Dotterel is a bird of the high mountain tops. In the Austrian Alps it has been found breeding above 7,500 feet; in the Riesengebirge above 5,000 feet; in the Cairngorms between 3,000 and 4,000 feet. It nests above the tree-line on stony plateaux where stunted heather, moss and lichen form the principal plant cover. That it should have colonized this area of Flevoland and be now breeding successfully five to ten feet below sea-level is one of the ornithological surprises of the century. Although we searched through binoculars until our eyes ached we could see no sign of them. Perhaps they had not yet arrived. In any case, for seeing Dotterels we could afford to bide our time. This bird stood high on our list of priorities for Lapland. If all went well we should run him to earth on some bleak hilltop in the far, far north. It was in fact four weeks later almost to the day that we found our Dotterels on the slopes of Mt. Aligas on the border of Finnish and Norwegian Lapland.

As we continued our journey the desolate wastes soon gave way to reed beds, and the further we progressed along the dyke road the more watery became the terrain. Finally we were skirting an endless shallow mere for mile upon mile with reed beds stretching away as far as the eye could see. Birds of the reed beds were always in evidence – Herons and Harriers, and Reed and Sedge and Savi's Warblers with their constant chitter-chatter. And where the land opened up a little there were God-wits and Avocets breeding. We had an entertaining photographic encounter with a pair of Godwits with running young close to the roadside. The ruddy-plumaged male perched on a fence-post a few yards away. Outlined against a blue sky and with a yellow mustard crop at his feet he made a splendid picture of defiance and concern. A count of Avocets was made as we journeyed slowly along one five-mile stretch of reed-fringed mere. Some two hundred and fifty birds were counted on this stretch alone.

Another successful Flevoland colonist that we noted on the soil banks of the retaining wall was the dandelion, now seeding by the million. If, at dispersal time, the parachutes were blown inland a serious weed problem could arise. Land reclamation on this vast scale poses many interesting and unusual problems. Our visit to East Flevoland, however, left us with an abiding impression that the Dutch people have a resilience and a resourcefulness in these matters, and an enlightened approach to ecology and conservation that is most heartening.

It was late in the afternoon when we eventually returned to our caravan to find the English party whom we had met on Texel now camping beside us. They had noted an occupied Stork's nest on a cartwheel on top of a pole in a village a few miles away, and this we must not miss seeing. We had a little difficulty in locating the village but eventually had the pleasure of seeing our first Netherlands Stork sitting on its lofty nest. It was a pleasure, too, to share the happiness and pride of the villagers in their nesting Storks whose presence conferred a sense of privilege and whose well-being was clearly everyone's concern.

Next morning we awoke early. It was 6 a.m. The day was warm and still, the sun already hot. We glanced out of the caravan window at the trees by the water's edge a hundred yards away. They seemed vague and insubstantial. We found we were peering through a curtain of filmy gauze, through a glimmering veil that hung, fold upon fold, upon the tranquil morning air. It was the glint and gleam of sunshine on a myriad whirring wings.

Flevoland was in an eruptive mood: gnats were on the wing, not in hundreds but in unnumbered millions. On this virgin land Nature was running riot. From a biological standpoint it was fascinating to witness a

103

population explosion actually occurring. From a human standpoint the experience was not without its tribulations. To put it mildly, a degree of discomfort was involved. Christopher Robin, we decided, had nothing on us. We had gnats in the eyes and the ears and the nose, and gnats in the hair, and – if we stayed here much longer – gnats-between-the-toes. Give us honest sand any day!

Mercifully these creatures did not bite or sting: they simply intimidated by sheer weight of numbers. A morning stroll outside the caravan had a sort of biblical quality. It was Egypt in the time of the Pharaohs . . . 'and all the dust of the earth became gnats throughout the land, and there were gnats on man and beast . . .' and, as far as we were concerned, on bread and butter, on eggs and bacon, on milk and cornflakes. We suddenly decided we had had our fill of Flevoland. Like the Children of Israel we were more than ready to depart. And always, just ahead, there lay another Promised Land.

Before leaving the Netherlands we wanted to sample a woodland reserve, and what better than Imbosh, an area the size of the New Forest, where wild boars roamed and where the rare Black Woodpecker could be found. We had been told that the wild boars were fed by the foresters and could be seen and photographed if due precautions were observed. The authorities deliberately discourage cars from entering the heart of the reserve by leaving the woodland rides rutted and rough-surfaced. If you have any respect for your springs or your tyres you leave your car on the outskirts and make an expedition into the interior on foot. We had the additional incubus of a caravan in tow.

We penetrated a few miles into the forest and savoured its general atmosphere, but we decided not to risk the inner rides and so had to forgo the pleasure of seeing wild boars and Black Woodpeckers.

Imbosh, however, provided us with one new bird – the Crested Tit. It seems strange that this most attractive member of the titmouse family, so widely distributed over Western Europe, should be confined in Britain to the Speyside area of Scotland.

Farewell to the Netherlands, and northward now, across into Western Germany at Noordham. The route looked singularly unpromising for the next few hours. In England one would hardly choose a motorway for a day's excursion into the countryside. For its natural history interest the Bremen–Hamburg autobahn held out about the same prospects as the M.1. As we had no conservation contacts hereabouts we decided to head for Denmark with all possible speed. A flat tyre compelled us to spend an uneasy night on a lay-by before Hamburg was reached, but the following day we reached Rostov and the Danish border. Once across the border we knew that if we ran into difficulties the delay of a day or two would not seriously inconvenience us. We should always be within an hour or two of some nature reserve that could be included in our itinerary.

9

Denmark – Ribe, Agger and the Vejlerne

WE SPENT the night on the holiday island of Romo
which we reached by crossing a three-mile causeway across mud flats on which a great many waders
were dibbling. The following morning we continued our
journey northwards as far as Ribe, a pleasant medieval
town with its red-brick cathedral and narrow cobbled
streets. Ribe was at one time a prosperous inland port,
but as the river silted up its sea trade diminished. It now
serves this extensive area of southern Denmark as a
market town. As one wanders through its narrow streets
today, past ancient buildings over which there broods an
all-pervading gentleness and mellow charm, it is difficult
to realize that this little town was a by-word for savage
justice in the Denmark of long ago. The penalty for
adulterating honey or milk was the severing of the
felon's right hand, and a gauntlet representing the
severed hand was perpetually hung up on the wall by
the city gate as a grim warning to all who passed.

But it was not because of its historical or architectural
interest that we were visiting Ribe, but because throughout Denmark it is known as the Stork Town. From the
cathedral tower we looked down on sleepy old houses
and were immediately aware of a number of large white

splashes on the roof-tops. In the centre of each was a dark circular mass of sticks – a Stork's nest. One or two were on large flat tiles placed on the chimney tops. Others were on wheel-like structures specially constructed on the roofs of buildings. One was on the top of a roadside tree that had been deliberately lopped so as to provide a flat elevated area suitable for a nesting Stork. The most attractive site of all was provided by a pinnacle of the Town Hall – surely the most photographed of all the Storks' nests in Denmark judging by its frequent occurrence in guide books and on postcards.

We asked a local shopkeeper how many nests there were and he thought about a dozen. There were more a few years ago, but fewer Storks were coming back from their winter quarters. It was thought that they may be eating locusts sprayed with insecticides, unintentional victims of an eradication campaign.

We spent three happy hours in Ribe, and discovered amongst other things that colour film could be purchased at only two-thirds of its cost in England – a subtle inducement to indulge in snapshotting on a rather more generous scale than we had hitherto considered permissible.

It was late afternoon before we resumed our journey north. We were tempted to halt at Tipperne, a famous Danish marshland area, winter refuge of forty thousand wild duck, and a good summer breeding haunt of Avocets, but we decided to press on to Thisted in the province of Jutland which was to be our base for the next week.

It was a very pleasant hundred miles of Denmark through which we passed between Ribe and Thisted.

107

The rich farmland eventually gave way to heather-clad heathland, and then sea-inlets appeared as we neared the Limfjord. Always on our left, to the west, lay the North Sea, but somewhere away to the right was the Kattegat leading to the Baltic Sea. And now before us lay this lovely, land-locked fjord – a hundred-mile stretch of waterway, studded with islands, and concealing under its grey-green waters the richest oyster-bed in Europe – an underwater treasury from which two million oysters are harvested every year.

Birds were not much in evidence as we passed through Jutland. Hoodies had now taken the place of Carrion Crows. A few Lapwings were scattered over the farm-land. Corn Buntings sang monotonously from the telephone wires, but few other birds were noticed. As we neared the north-western tip of Jutland we entered Viking country. Ancient burial mounds appeared with increasing frequency along the skyline. And so, on a cool and windy evening, we entered Thisted, found the municipal caravan site, and drew off the tarmac on to a green lawn fronting the Limfjord. We were immediately given a very warm welcome by the Warden and his wife who confirmed the impression that we had already received since entering this country that we were now in the land of 'the friendly Danes'.

What of this country in which we were now installed, its size and the agricultural background against which any conservation efforts would have to be measured? Denmark, the smallest of the Scandinavian countries, consists of the long peninsula of Jutland, and five hundred islands about a fifth of which are inhabited. Ninety-two per cent of its soil is under cultivation.

Denmark is, in fact, all farm, although the individual farm units are not large. The average Danish farmer, helped by his wife and a single farm hand, works some thirty-seven acres from which he produces enough food annually to feed between eighty and ninety people. He is the only farmer in the western world to do this, and he does it without government subsidies and without protection against foreign competition. He does it by sheer hard work and efficiency, and by joining with other farmers in co-operative enterprises. The Danes found many years ago that they were obliged to co-operate if they were to compete in the world market, and hence their highly efficient co-operative dairies, pig factories, egg-marketing and export associations. It was towards the end of the last century when cheap grain from the prairies of the New World began to lower the selling price of European corn that Denmark realized she must change from a corn-producing to a dairy-farming economy.

Over a million of Denmark's four and a half million inhabitants live in and around Copenhagen. Apart from this one major conurbation the population is evenly spread over its sixteen and a half million square miles. With two hundred and seventy inhabitants to the square mile Denmark has only a quarter of the population density of the Netherlands.

Only eight per cent of Danish soil is not under cultivation, and this consists of heath, dune and open bog. Extensive forests of deciduous trees at one time covered much of Denmark but few remnants survive, though there are enough trees scattered individually over the landscape not to give it a bare or denuded appearance.

Reafforestation is taking place in the dune-lands on the north-western coastal strip. With the high value placed on land for farming purposes the only areas that can be spared for conservation are those that are agriculturally non-productive. Denmark has a long Atlantic coast-line comparatively unfrequented except for recreational purposes during the brief summer season. It is on the coastal shingles, on the dunes, and in the marshlands behind the dunes that much of Denmark's richness of bird life is to be found. It was in just such an area, near to the little fishing village of Agger, that we were to have our most enjoyable bird-watching during our stay in Jutland.

We spent the morning after our arrival at Thisted in exploring the town, sending off films to be processed, and collecting 'Poste-Restante' letters – which included permits from Professor Sparck of the 'Naturfrednings-radet' for visits to the Tipperne and Vejlerne reserves. In the afternoon we set forth to explore the Agger Tange, a five-mile marshy peninsula behind the dunes on the western coast. Even at a distance we could sense that it had all the ingredients for good bird-watching. Sheltered by the dunes on one side, and flanked by a broad expanse of water on the other it looked full of promise. A careful sweep of the binoculars disclosed a hundred and fifty Avocets, many of them sitting on nests, and a flock of eighty Pink-footed Geese grazing unconcernedly in the wet meadows. It was interesting to reflect that these would be Spitzbergen-breeding birds and not geese of the Icelandic race that we see each winter in the Lincolnshire fenlands. Black-headed Gulls were brawling in a distant gallery, and Black-tailed

Godwits, Dunlins, Snipe and Redshanks were plentifully in evidence. The Agger Tange was clearly one of the richest bird haunts we had yet discovered – if only the weather would improve. At the moment the marsh was cold and wind-swept, and we were reluctant to spend any length of time exploring because of the danger of chilling the eggs of any birds disturbed from their nests in this open country.

As we left the car a Redshank leapt from its nest in a deep tussock a few paces from the road. There were photographic possibilities here that we noted for future reference. We had a brief wander over the marsh and quickly found three Avocets' nests within twenty yards of each other. A pair of Dunlins trilled apprehensively by the edge of a pool. They were almost certainly nesting in the vicinity, but it was not fair to carry out an intensive search in these chilling conditions.

Back at the caravan site we began laying plans for the morrow. The Agger marshes had been most rewarding. Now for the Vejlerne. Our interest in this reserve had been aroused by a chapter in Alan Davidson's book *A Bird Watcher in Scandinavia*. He had visited the Vejlerne in former days when it was a private shooting reserve staunchly keepered by a formidable character who was liable to discharge his twelve-bore at the retreating posteriors of trespassers surprised on his marsh. His cartridges were loaded not with lead shot but with fragmented rock-salt crystals guaranteed to sting in the memory and elsewhere for a long time afterwards. Although we were armed with a written permit bearing Professor Sparck's signature we felt it would be unwise to take unnecessary chances. A preliminary telephone call was not only a matter of courtesy: it was one of discretion. The Warden at the caravan site volunteered to act on our behalf. He soon returned with the excellent news that the keeper had already been informed by Professor Sparck of our impending visit. We were free to enter the reserve at any time without the necessity of making contact with the keeper. The Vejlerne was all ours.

The word 'vejlerne' in Danish means 'marshland', but graced with a capital V it refers to this vast area of reedy meres and flooded fenland to the north-east of Thisted that now forms the finest nature reserve in the whole of Denmark. At the beginning of the present century this area was dammed off from the Limfjord in an abortive attempt at land reclamation. When the plan did not succeed the resulting marshy wilderness was given over to wildlife. It is no exaggeration to say that the Vejlerne has now become for Denmark what the Camargue is for the south of France – a naturalists' paradise.

Determined on an early start we had a six o'clock breakfast the following morning. Patches of blue sky were showing but the wind was unusually keen for mid-May. From the caravan windows we looked out over a clipped hedge at the sparkling waters of the Limfjord. As we breakfasted a dapper, male Pied Flycatcher came flitting along the hedge: it seemed a good omen with which to start off the day.

We decided to approach the Vejlerne from the south by a rough road that ran along the containing dam at this point. Our progress was slow, not because of the rough state of the road, but because frequent halts were made so that we could become better acquainted with the birds

112

out on the marshland. Greylag Geese were grazing watchfully in the lush meadows. Avocets, Black-tailed Godwits and Oyster-Catchers were in nesting territories in the partially-flooded fields. Where there were pools Black-headed Gulls were nesting in noisy communities. Common Gulls were nesting singly or in twos and threes; and, hawking for insects along the waterways were lovely, graceful Black Terns. Half a mile away where the green of the marsh gave way to the gold of the reed beds and the blue of distant water we could see more birds on the wing – more gulls, more Black Terns, and, from time to time, the dark winnowing wings of a Marsh Harrier. There, too, we knew that every year a few pairs of Spoonbills – the only ones nesting in Denmark – made their nests.

After three miles of fruitful meandering along the top of the dam we took a rough road northwards, but it grew impossibly narrow after half a mile, and we felt it would be foolhardy to proceed further. We had already located three Ruffs' tilting-grounds out in the marsh. Godwits yelped at us all the way. Many had running young and we were fortunate to find a young Godwit, a few hours old, crossing the track just ahead of us. We filmed him as he staggered uncertainly along the rutted road.

We had lunch overlooking a shallow pool where Ringed Plovers, Dunlins, Little Stints and a Curlew Sandpiper in russet breeding plumage all fed unconcernedly some twenty yards away. After lunch we made a circuit of the entire Vejlerne area, and re-entered the reserve from the north. We wanted to discover the track described by Alan Davidson which, for two or three

miles, passed through a continuous Black-headed Gullery where some twenty-five thousand birds were nesting. We followed his itinerary as best we could, but
apart from one small colony of less than a hundred pairs
we drew a blank. We returned to the pumping mill near
to the entrance to the reserve and encountered two
young Danish ornithologists there. They confirmed that
we had been in the right place for the gullery of former
years but said that for no known reason the gulls had
forsaken it. Some two to three thousand now nested in
the flooded grasslands and by the reedy meres where we
had seen them earlier in the day. We asked about the
rare Little Gulls that Alan Davidson had found breeding
here. Yes, they were still breeding in the reserve –
about fifteen pairs of them – and they were just starting
to nest. As we were talking, a small black-capped gull
with dusky undersides to its rounded wings came flying
overhead. The young Danes were delighted to point it
out to us. We asked them about another Veljerne
speciality, the Gull-billed Tern. A few were still here
but they were less common than in former years. The
Black Terns that were hawking for insects along the
waterways would have nests in about a week's time. A
shallow part of the mere where they would make their
floating platforms was pointed out to us, and through
the binoculars we could see a score of birds hovering
over the water-weeds or alighting on herbage there.
Four pairs of Spoonbills had reared families last year,
and they had returned again this year. Marsh Harriers
were still fairly plentiful, but Montagu's Harriers nesting
on nearby heathland less so. We inquired of other
interesting localities in the neighbourhood, and were

114

told of a wood and heathland area a few miles away to the north-west where two pairs of Golden Plovers nested last year and where Wood-Sandpipers also bred.

We still had a couple of hours daylight left, so we set forth to explore this heathland before sundown. We found it without difficulty and spent an hour slogging back and forth in the biting wind across that blasted heath but all to no purpose. We returned to the caravan cold, hungry and a little dispirited, but generous helpings of hot soup and tinned steak soon restored morale. During the night the wind increased, and with a full gale blowing at dawn, we decided not to venture far afield but to spend the morning in Thisted and wait for the weather to improve. After lunch, although the sun came out, a searing wind continued to make any outdoor activity distinctly uncomfortable. To seek a more sheltered spot we visited a newly-afforested region in the north-west corner of Jutland. We wandered through avenues of pines, dark and sombre, and sighing in the wind. Apart from Chaffinches the woods seemed singularly devoid of birds. We finally decided to brave the wind and pay another visit to the Agger marshes. At least we could have a shot at the Redshank from the shelter of the car. On arriving there we carefully drew the car off the road and halted it a few paces from the nest. Having installed my brother behind the curtained windows, my task was to flush the sitting Redshank from her nest and then withdraw for half an hour. The entrance to the Avocet marsh was not far away and I reckoned on having a quarter of an hour there before having to return, but almost immediately I stumbled across an Avocet's nest with downy young that simply

115

had to be photographed, and then a pair of Dunlins began behaving most suspiciously and inviting a search for their nest. And so the minutes slipped by, and when I finally returned to the car a full hour had passed and a very disgruntled brother was waiting in the car interior.

The Redshank had returned in five minutes – and returned so hurriedly that he had missed her going on to the nest. For the remaining fifty-five minutes he had crouched there in growing discomfort and mounting impatience while I was gaily gallivanting in the marshes. It took a full quarter of an hour to quench his ire and restore his circulation, and it was not until he was kneeling beside the family of baby Avocets in the marsh that his customary good humour returned.

The wind moderated overnight and we spent the following day filming the Black-headed Gulls at the Vejlerne, and also in paying a late afternoon visit to the Agger marshes where the Redshank was finally filmed and photographed without any further contretemps. We visited the southern extremity of this marshy peninsula and watched two Short-eared Owls hunting, and surprised eighteen Red-breasted Mergansers from a lonely pool. We also watched a partially albino Oyster-catcher displaying to another bird that appeared to be its mate. Unlike the pure white Oyster-catcher we had seen on Texel this bird had startingly black tips to the primary feathers on its wings. It was, in fact, an Oyster-catcher with the plumage of a Stork – a very elegant and handsome bird.

Our week in Thisted with the friendly Danes passed all too quickly. We liked Thisted as a town: it was a comfortable size and so very pleasantly situated, looking south over the ever-changing waters of the Limfjord and north and west over undulating meadows dotted with tumuli. And, of course, to the east lay the riches of the Veljerne. It was pleasant to see old customs being observed – the local chimney sweep riding by on his bicycle and wearing the traditional top hat, and the postmen in their livery of hunting pink.

In the heart of the town a beautiful old church stood in a quiet churchyard where Collared Doves were nesting in the tall trees. Inside the church the roof-vaulting was a replica in stone of the timbered structure of some ancient moot-hall, and on the walls were vast, commemorative medallions with ornate gilded scrollwork surrounding centre portrait-panels. The most impressive of these was over three hundred years old and showed a pastor in full clerical dress identical as far as we could judge with that of the present incumbent. There was also a very old and beautiful hexagonal pulpit intricately carved and painted, and dating from the end of the sixteenth century. It was interesting to reflect that while an unknown craftsman here in Jutland was chiselling from Danish oak this little masterpiece for Thisted church, another craftsman in a different medium was fashioning a masterpiece of creative writing just over the water on English soil. And yet, in a sense, both had Danish origins. This beautiful old pulpit and *Hamlet*, *Prince of Denmark* were almost exact contemporaries.

Our stay in Thisted was drawing to a close, but there were one or two investigations still to be made. In the villages bordering the Vejlerne – at Veslos, Osterild and Frostrup – there were three Storks' nests to be discovered. One, we found, was on the roof of a local 'kro' or hotel – a fairly orthodox situation. The other two were on more interesting sites: they were on telegraph poles near the village centres. In Denmark, wherever a junction of telephone wires occurs, a box-like structure of wooden struts is created on top of a telegraph pole. This provides an admirable platform on which Storks can build a nest, though to what extent their nesting activities interfere with telephonic communications throughout Jutland is a matter for conjecture. The nest at Frostrup had additional tenants in the basement. A pair of Starlings and several House Sparrows were occupying adjacent flats in the lower levels of the nest.

One of our most happy bird-watching experiences came on our last afternoon in Jutland when we paid a final visit to the fishing village of Agger and its adjacent marshes. Many bird memories are vivid and pleasurable because of the rarity of the subject that has come under observation. Our pleasure on this sunny afternoon was bestowed by the commonest of all bird species – the ubiquitous Starling, as abundant in Jutland as in most parts of Britain. We know from ringing returns that vast numbers of Starlings wintering in Britain are birds of continental origin. The rings on their legs prove that they have been reared in countries around the Baltic Sea – but where do they find holes in which to rear their families? Here, in Agger and similar villages, had we but realized it, was the answer to that question. Already when passing through Danish villages we had often noted Starling nesting-boxes nailed to cottage walls. Now, in Agger, we decided to have a closer look – and we were astonished and delighted by what we found. There were nesting-boxes everywhere. Every cottage boasted its Starling mansion. Some were rough and ready affairs nailed to cottage walls five or six feet above ground level. Others were more elaborate residences, erected on poles and containing four or five separate compartments. Gaily painted and with the Danish flag proudly flying, they made charming additions to cottage gardens. Again and again we noted, from the frequent comings and goings of tenants, that ground floor, first floor and attic rooms were in simultaneous occupation. Several of these residences had fanciful additions that might well have had a discouraging effect on prospective tenants elsewhere – a windmill with sails slowly turning – a little gyrating wooden soldier with limbs that jerked alarmingly with every gust of wind. But in their domestic arrangements the Agger Starlings had acquired a remarkable sophistication. They seemed not in the least deterred by such frivolity. Unquestionably the most attractive of all the Agger Starling mansions were those constructed from disused fishing buoys. These slender cones, brightly painted in the national colours of red and white, were erected on tall poles, and usually several pairs of birds were in residence. It was fortunate that we had arrived in Agger at the peak of the nesting season. In all these Starling homes there were families clamouring to be fed.

For nearly two hours we moved about the village with cameras on tripods, photographing and filming to our heart's content. The local inhabitants viewed our activities with tolerance and undisguised amusement. They were clearly surprised that we should consider this passion of theirs for erecting Starling mansions as in any way unusual. For the Danes the Starling is the harbinger of spring, and they try to ensure that a warm welcome awaits it on returning from winter quarters in England's green and pleasant land.

During our last two days in Denmark the weather had improved beyond belief. The sun now shone from a cloudless sky: the wind had dropped, and, for the first time since leaving Flevoland we could doff pullovers and anoraks and put on summer wear. Farewell then to Thisted, and now the road to Frederikshaven, with mile upon mile of heathland along the golden roads of Jutland – golden with dandelions in their millions along the roadside verges. Dandelions are the 'danegeld' of modern Denmark. Their abundance results from the current passion for road improvement. Danish roads, we were told, are the second best in Europe. First place was grudgingly conceded to France. But, with all this road-widening in progress, new roadside verges are all the time being created, and the first successful colonist is almost invariably the dandelion. Exceptions occurred and occasionally we would see ahead of us what at first appeared to be a patch of blue sky or a sheet of blue water by the side of the road. A closer view disclosed a dense carpet of blue wild pansies. As colonists they had beaten the dandelions to it by a short stalk.

We passed meadows sprinkled with cowslips and were reminded of meadows similarly adorned in France when we began our journey five weeks ago. Cherries and pears were blossoming in the orchards but apple blossom was still at the pink-bud stage. Wood anemones – pale, fragile windflowers – lay in drifts in the roadside cuttings. By the tokens of spring we were still, by our accustomed standards, at about mid-April. Botanically, north Jutland was a full month behind the English calendar. It was a pleasing confirmation that we were indeed travelling north with the spring. Here, in Jutland, the hounds of spring were still on winter's traces. Reluctant summer was still far, far away in the south: we were, as yet, in no danger of being overtaken.

10

A Week in Southern Sweden

THE surface of the Kattegat was smooth and unruffled as we made our crossing in brilliant sunshine from Frederikshaven to Gothenburg. There are not many days in the year when there is neither wind nor wave on these narrow, troubled waters. We were accompanied by a host of gulls, but we noted with interest that there were more Lesser Black-backed than Herring Gulls in the slip-stream of our slow and stately-moving ferry – perhaps an indication that we were now in more northern waters.

We searched the outskirts of Gothenburg for a cara-van site, and found, in the southern suburbs, more by accident than design, a delightful pear orchard that looked as though it could house a caravan without inconvenience for a few days. I went to the nearby house and knocked on the door. The daughter of the house appeared and stood there, tall and fair and smiling, in the doorway. 'Welcome to Sweden,' she seemed to say. But surely I had seen her before – or did all girls in Sweden look like Ingrid Bergman? 'We are from England,' I said, speaking slowly and carefully so that if she spoke English she would understand. 'We are visiting Sweden. May we bring our caravan here, under the trees, for a few days?' She was a little startled when she heard the English tongue but quickly regained her composure. 'I will ask,' she said, and disappeared indoors. In a few moments she returned. 'Yes,' she said. 'Over there, under the trees. You will find hot and cold water in the building nearby. You are very welcome.' And so, in this first brief but charming encounter we discovered Sweden. This little incident epitomized for us the welcome that we were everywhere to receive in this friendly land. The Swedes were rather more serious and certainly more reserved than the Danes but their friendliness was never in doubt.

For a visitor the first fact about Sweden that must be grasped is that of size. Sweden is a very large country. It has nearly twice the land area of the British Isles and yet it has only a seventh of its population. The impression of size increases when considered in terms of length and breadth. From its southern shore to the north of Swedish Lapland the distance is little short of a thousand miles. We knew that when we left Gothenburg and headed for Haparanda at the head of the Bothnian Gulf we faced a long haul of eight hundred miles. To reach the Arctic Sea by way of Finnish Lapland another three hundred miles of gravelled roads awaited us.

But before leaving for Lapland we proposed spending a few days in central and southern Sweden. We wanted to get the feel of the country, and we had a fine map and booklet supplied by the Svenska Naturskyddsforeningen – the Swedish Society for Nature Conservation – which listed 346 conservation areas, several of them within reach of Gothenburg. It was a matter for regret that it seemed unlikely with the limited time at our disposal that we should be able to visit any of the sixteen National Parks that are a source of great pride to the people of Sweden. These include several wonderful, wild regions north of the Arctic Circle in Swedish Lapland – Sarek, Abisco and Muddus – which represent some of the wildest and most primitive landscapes in Europe today. Here some fifteen thousand square miles of territory have been declared a National Park. In addition, throughout the length and breadth of Sweden there are great numbers of bird and animal sanctuaries established by Royal Proclamation, and the area of land so 'protected' now amounts to over two thousand square miles. As well as birds and mammals, plants come in for special protective measures. This is not altogether surprising in a country which produced one of the most eminent botanists and natural historians of all time. The name Linnaeus is held in honour not only in Gothenburg but the world over. In Sweden quite small areas, and natural objects of special historical, aesthetic or biological interest, can be set aside. Many of these are individual trees of great age or splendour. With timber the acknowledged 'green gold' of Sweden and its neighbours the particular interest in trees is understandable.

Geologically, Sweden owes much of its rugged grandeur to the ancient rocks that underlie its forest lands. Valleys and hollows scoured by glaciation from the hard, impervious rocks of the 'Baltic Shield' give rise to lakes and tarns innumerable. It is an exciting prospect for the fisherman who enjoys sampling sport in as wide a variety of waters as possible that there are no less than ninety-five thousand lakes in Sweden. If he were to fish ten different lakes a day, every day of the year, it would take him twenty-six years to cover them all.

We proposed at the first opportunity to do an inland tour of the lakeland country within reach of Gothenburg, but meanwhile we must establish ourselves in our little pear orchard and take the measure of the natural history in our immediate neighbourhood. It was while preparing supper in the caravan that we made our first observation. Looking out from the caravan windows we noticed a pair of thrushes hopping around in the orchard grass collecting food. They were stuffing their beaks with worms and clearly had a nest near at hand. They were behaving in exactly the same way as would a pair of Song Thrushes in England, and they had the same degree of unconcern in the presence of humans. But these were not Song Thrushes. They were bigger and greyer, and their alarm note was a loud 'flack...flack'. They were northern thrushes – Fieldfares. We could hardly have had a more appropriate reminder of our new geographical situation. Even here we were on the threshold of the arctic. Increasingly from now onwards the fauna and flora would be different. A further reminder came during supper when the Fieldfares showed a sudden concern, and flew off with jarring alarm-notes to mob a Hooded Crow that had alighted on a nearby tree. With incessant harsh cries they proceeded to attack the intruder. But the Hoodie stuck its ground, croaking continuously and menacingly at the Fieldfares. It was not on a raiding expedition, we discovered, but was racked with parental anxiety because one of its young, just out of the nest, was fluttering in the undergrowth near the Fieldfares' nest. For ten minutes the din continued – and was duly recorded on 'tape' – before the young Hoodie extracted itself and flew unsteadily out of the Fieldfares' territory and into the comparative safety of a nearby spinney.

After supper we made contact with our sole neighbour in the pear orchard, a Swedish engineer whose caravan was drawn up close to ours. He spoke English fluently and had been to England for a family holiday the previous year. He gave us many useful hints on caravanning in Sweden, and stressed that from now onwards our nomadic existence would be all the more pleasurable for being lived against the background of the so-called 'Individual Rights' in Sweden. These imply that anyone is at liberty to cross any ground, cultivated or otherwise. providing that no direct harm will result. You have the right to camp beside the highway or in a forest clearing, or by a lakeside; you can bathe in lakes and rivers; you can pick wild berries and mushrooms, and enjoy the free recreational values of the countryside wherever you may be. In theory there is no such thing as 'Trespassers will be Prosecuted' in the whole of Sweden. The countryside belongs to the people. Courtesy and good manners should ensure that privileges on this generous scale will not be abused. It is obviously inconsiderate to pitch a tent in someone's back garden, or to stride across a hay meadow just ready for cutting, but if good sense and good manners are displayed, the whole of Sweden is yours to explore without let or hindrance. It stands to reason that this enlightened attitude is far more possible in a country that averages forty-three inhabitants to the square mile than it would be in Britain where the population density is twelve times as great.

The following morning I awoke at 2.30 a.m. It was

already getting light and the Dawn Chorus was beginning. Against a general background of 'thrush-blackbird'
song were other new and interesting notes, and one that
was particularly intriguing – a 'zeu...zeu...zeu...zeu...
zee...zee...' call that I was hoping to hear – the song of
the Ortolan Bunting. A Redstart perched on a spray of
blossoming pear was also singing away to the best of its
limited ability, and presently it darted down and disappeared into a crevice in the loosely-constructed wall
that formed the orchard boundary.

After breakfast and a brief shopping expedition into
Gothenburg we set forth to explore the countryside and
discover our first Swedish lake. In the environs of
Gothenburg the farmland was similar in character to
that of northern Denmark. Spring ploughing was taking
place and gulls were in attendance, but there were more
northern-nesting Common Gulls than 'Black-heads'.

We found our lake, a hollow in the granite hills,
fringed with silver birch and alder, and very lovely in the
spring sunshine. For three miles we bumped our way
along the gravel road by the lakeside looking for water
birds without success. But on a sandy beach at the far end
we spied two birds that held out interesting possibilities.
They were dark-looking sandpipers with prominent
white rumps, and when they took to the air with clear
'tweet...weet...weet' cries and looking like oversized
House Martins we knew that they were Green Sandpipers. It was not too early for them to be nesting – an
exciting prospect because of the originality they show
in their choice of nesting-site. It was just over a century
ago that Professor Newton, an eminent ornithologist of
his day, made known to an incredulous British public the

newly-discovered fact that the Green Sandpiper habitually lays its eggs in the old nest of a Song Thrush, Blackbird or Fieldfare, or even on a Wood Pigeon's flimsy platform of sticks. The only other European wader that will occasionally do this is the Wood-Sandpiper when the low-lying forests it frequents are flooded.

Miss M. D. Haviland, a pioneer photographer of the birds of sub-arctic regions, once described an encounter with a tree-nesting bird of this species. 'I was climbing up to what appeared to be a Fieldfare's nest, when, unexpectedly, a long beak like a bee's sting darted over the brim, and instead of the original architect, the grey poll of a Wood-Sandpiper popped up.'

If only we could repeat the experience with the Green Sandpiper! We searched an alder thicket near to where the birds had been feeding, but to no avail, and so we proceeded on our way. Another half-mile and a sandpiper of a different species fluttered away from the lakeside herbage as we rattled past. It was a Common Sandpiper, an old friend of our boyhood days whose nest we had found on the banks of the River Dove. Its nest with a full clutch of four handsome eggs was concealed amongst dead leaves and early green herbage between the lake and the road which were not ten yards apart at this point. As a discovery it lacked the distinction that would have attended the finding of a Green Sandpiper's nest, but it was a pleasant consolation prize. Furthermore we could, with any luck, sit quietly in the car and watch the bird return, filming and photographing her as she did so. A happy hour's photography followed, and as well as the sandpiper we had for company beside

A disused fishing buoy makes a fine
Starling mansion.   Agger, Jutland.

5   From the observation tower at Varnamo,
                          S. Sweden, Cranes can be seen nesting in the
                          distant marshland.

Wood-Sandpiper returning to its nest.
Finnish Lapland.

6

Red-necked Phalaropes – courtship display
on an arctic pool.   Karigasniemi.

that Swedish lake a pair of Pied Flycatchers, a Great
Spotted Woodpecker and a very cheerful Nuthatch. We
returned to our pear orchard well pleased with our first
impression of Sweden.

The following day, Thursday, was Ascension Day,
observed in Sweden as a whole holiday, with Friday,
Saturday and Sunday thrown in for good measure. All
Sweden was in festive mood and the weather matched
the occasion. We proposed to extend our explorations
by going on safari for a couple of days to Varnamo in the
Southern Swedish Uplands. This would entail a night
away from the caravan, sleeping rough and cooking on
wood fires, but it was worth a little discomfort to have
the chance of visiting a marshy area that possessed
unique features on account of its peculiar elevation. It
was, in effect, a pocket of Lapland in southern Sweden.
The fact that it was a mere few hundred feet above the
surrounding countryside meant that birds of sub-arctic
regions could be found breeding there.

A leisurely hundred-mile journey through the Swedish
countryside gave us the opportunity of assessing the
variety and frequency of farmland and hedgerow birds in
this region. Starlings and Chaffinches were plentiful, and
Fieldfares as common as Blackbirds and Song Thrushes.
White Wagtails (the continental version of our Pied
Wagtail) were trotting by all the lakesides, and Red-
starts appeared in stone-wall country, and Whinchats on
rough hillsides. Wood Pigeons were conspicuous by
their absence: in two hundred miles of travel we saw
only four pairs of these birds. Yellow Hammers were
seldom seen, although it appeared to be good Yellow
Hammer country. Robins seemed shy: we seldom saw

one but their song was often heard. As in Denmark we noticed many Starling mansions erected in cottage gardens, but we hardly expected to find no less than twenty-eight nesting-boxes in one colony alone. They were all on silver birches beside a lake, and were sited so that all their entrance-holes faced a little chalet by the lakeside. How pleasant to be able to watch, from your chalet windows, twenty-eight pairs of Starlings in zealous occupation of the homes that you have provided for them. We tried to convey this sentiment to the owner of the chalet who came out to watch us filming the birds, but it was a conversation conducted entirely in gesture. This elderly Starling enthusiast was not bilingual, but he appreciated our interest in his birds, gesticulating expansively and smiling in a very friendly and co-operative way.

It was on this journey, as we traversed the lovely Swedish lakeland, that we discovered Swedish gold – the gold of kingcups fringing the lake shores. We passed a score of lakes, each one a burnished shield of azure edged with gold.

It was evening when we reached Varnamo, and, equipped only with a large-scale map, we had some difficulty in finding the exact location of the upland 'moss'. We wandered for an hour or more along rutted gravel lanes, past timbered farmhouses painted, Swedish-fashion, dark blood-red and white. At last, in the deep dusk, we came out on to high level ground. We halted the car, switched off the engine and listened. The air was alive with the cries of marshland birds. Bubbling calls of Curlews mingled with the tremulous bleat of drumming Snipe, and, out on the marsh, a new cry was

sounding, a clear and musical 'tinka...tinka...tinka...
tinka–tink'. Bells were tinkling in the boglands. This
must be the bird the Danes call the 'Tinksmed' – the
Wood-Sandpiper. Ahead of us, by the side of the road,
was a copse and an area of fenced grassland on to which
we could draw the car away from the road. A sign could
be dimly discerned in the gathering darkness. It said
'Fagelskyddsplats' – 'Bird Reserve'. We were there.

A footpath led away towards the edge of the marsh.
Although we could see only a few yards we had a com-
pelling urge to follow the path and see where it led. A
strange new cry urged us on. It was a curious plangent,
whiplash call with an extraordinary carrying effect. We
thought at first that it came from a bird about thirty
yards ahead – a new species of owl perhaps – but as we
made our way forwards it was always ahead of us, and
when we arrived at the edge of the marsh it was still out
there in the bogland itself. Where the grassland ended
and the marsh began, a group of tall pines stood darkly
silhouetted against the night sky. As we approached we
became aware of a massive wooden structure rearing its
huge bulk from within the pines and o'ertopping them
by a clear eight or ten feet. It was an observation tower,
and we could dimly see two figures standing on the
platform at the top, motionless and listening. Presently
I became aware of a third silent figure standing less than
ten yards away at the foot of the tower. I approached and
almost in a whisper I questioned him about the identity
of the 'whiplash' bird. He was a little startled at being
addressed in a foreign tongue, but he recovered and
replied in faltering English that he knew the bird but
was not familiar with its English name. His friends who

were up the tower had a bird book with English names and they would tell me when they came down. While this whispered conversation had been taking place I became aware of another extraordinary sound coming this time from the dark sky above. 'Lok-toggi…lok-toggi…lok-toggi…lok-toggi.' Hollow hoof-beats were ringing out with a rhythmic urgency as a ghostly horse-man went cantering by through the darkened vault of heaven. My thoughts flew to John Wolley and his description of the Jack Snipe's nuptial song. Over a century ago he had put on record for the first time a description of this remarkable sound: 'At the time I could not at all guess what it was, an extraordinary sound unlike anything I had heard before. I could not tell from what direction it came, and it filled me with a curious suspense. My Finnish interpreter thought it was a Capercaillie and at the time I could not contradict him; but soon I found it was a small bird gliding at a wild pace at a great height over the marsh. I know not how better to describe the noise than by likening it to the cantering of a horse in the distance over a hard, hollow road: it came in fours, with a similar cadence and a like clear, yet hollow sound.' I was to hear this extraordinary sound again in Lapland. It was one of the recurring themes of our northward journey, but I could not have wished for a better setting for my first introduction than the one in which I found myself now. In retrospect I think that, musically, this was the most exciting moment of the trip. For years I had known about this curious 'song', and had longed to hear it. At Varnamo marsh in the Southern Swedish Uplands, towards midnight, the wish had been fulfilled.

132

We returned from the marsh to the car with the three young Swedes. They were students from the University of Gothenburg, and they were on their way to an ornithological convention in the south. The 'whiplash' bird, still calling stridently from the marshes, was identified as a Spotted Crake.

We looked at bird books and maps together by torchlight on the bonnet of the car. A common interest in wildlife and a common concern about its conservation drew us closely together and the language barrier was easily surmounted. Much of the talk centred on toxic chemicals and their devastating effects on wildlife. Many birds in Sweden, they said, were being 'intoxicated'. In farming districts the Yellow Hammer had almost disappeared. Wood Pigeons and Rooks were diminishing dramatically, but the birds of prey, as in other countries, were the worst affected, coming as they do at the end of a food chain. Sea Eagles on the Norwegian coast had seriously declined in numbers, and Golden Eagles were being affected inland. Kestrels, once abundant, were now quite scarce. The effect on Sparrow Hawks was not yet very noticeable but no doubt that would follow. Ospreys were diminishing and laboratory tests on dead birds found beside Lake Vattern had established beyond doubt that toxic chemicals were the cause of death. In Sweden the indiscriminate use of the deadly organophosphates was far too widespread. It was even now occurring in eggs laid by domestic poultry and Swedes were officially being advised to limit their consumption of these. Two items on the credit side were that Turnstones, normally maritime birds, were now nesting inland on islets on the great lakes; and a pair of

Whooper Swans and several pairs of Cranes were this year nesting in the great marsh of Varnamo.

It was now past midnight and time for us to say a reluctant farewell to these enthusiastic young conservationists. A few hundred men like these scattered over Sweden in the years that lay ahead would, we felt, exert a beneficial influence that could be powerful indeed.

Although it was already long past normal bedtime we felt we could not miss the opportunity of hearing a Swedish marshland Dawn Chorus, so the alarm clock was set for 2.30 a.m., and we scrambled into our sleeping bags for a couple of hours' rest. The alarm clock was unnecessary after all. Shortly before it was due to go off, a weird honking and clanging started up in the distant marshland. It was the 'trucking' cry of Cranes indulging in their courtship display, and, nearer at hand, there now came the curious, continuous bubbling and grunting of a Blackcock on a 'lek'. The sound was coming from the roadside two hundred yards away. We went along to investigate, and there he was – a magnificent cock bird, with jet black wings and tail stiffly spread, white rump gleaming and red wattles glowing – a noble sight. Presently he flew away a short distance and alighted on the top of a five-foot silver birch from which he continued to display his defiance, looking most impressively belligerent up there.

When the light improved we climbed the observation tower and scanned the marshland for birds. There were waders everywhere and a fair sprinkling of ducks and gulls, but the birds that arrested our attention appeared as dark specks in the distance – two, and then two more – and then odd ones here and there. We counted nine

134

birds in all. We were watching Cranes in the wild for the first time, and from the lofty elevation of the observation tower we could see that three at least were sitting on nests.

What an excellent idea is the watch tower! Here in the Varnamo marsh there is no resident warden in charge. There are no 'excursies' over the marshland. From April to August it is inviolate. But all day long visitors come from near and far to climb the tower so that they may watch the distant birds without disturbing them. An excursion out on that sphagnum bog would, in any case, be a hazardous enterprise. You could soon be up to your thighs in cold, peaty water and get into serious difficulties. But without the tower many a visitor would be tempted out into the marsh if only to discover what was there. But the tower removes the need for such foolhardiness. You climb it and are satisfied: the riches of Varnamo are spread before your eyes.

On the return journey to Gothenburg we passed more lovely lakes on four of which we saw pairs of Black-throated Divers. We had another fruitless search for a Green Sandpiper's nest, but again found a Common Sandpiper's while searching for its rarer cousin's nesting site. We noted many duck nesting-boxes, intended for Goldeneyes, attached to lakeside trees, and on more than one occasion we saw a possible tenant swimming nearby or flying past.

We arrived back at our pear orchard in the cool of the evening tired but contented. We had had two wonderfully interesting days – with a two-hour night between. It was good training for what lay in store in Lapland.

Our last two days at Gothenburg were spent in making fairly gentle excursions into the surrounding countryside. We were really marking time waiting for my son Tim to arrive from Tilbury so that he might join us for the Lapland venture. We were also, in a sense, gathering strength for the long haul north. Haparanda, where we entered Lapland, was more than eight hundred miles away and we hoped to cover the distance in three days.

We met Tim at the Gothenburg docks at 6.30 a.m. on the last day of May and returned to the pear orchard for breakfast. We had a final sorting-out and stowage of gear, and we said our farewells to the kindly Swedish family who had allowed us to use their orchard for the past week. We returned to Gothenburg for the laying-in of provisions for the journey, and for booking our return passage to England in four or five weeks' time. But we received a set-back. All accommodation on Swedish boats to England was already booked up to mid-August. It looked as though, at the end of June, we should have to face the hard slog back through Denmark, Western Germany, Holland, Belgium and into France to queue up at Calais or Dieppe for a cancellation crossing to our homeland. This was a blow, but we were in no mood to let a set-back of this kind detract from the pleasure of our journey to the north. No doubt a military strategist would refuse to advance without first securing his line of retreat, but this was a holiday venture not an army campaign. At least we would not now be dogged by the necessity of returning to Gothenburg at a fixed date. It was almost with a feeling of relief that we finally set forth, just after midday, and headed north-east for the distant Baltic shore. We kept at it steadily for the next seven hours with only a couple of halts for refreshment. In Denmark we had discovered the sustaining virtues of 'Varme Polsers' – 'Hot Dogs' served with tomato sauce, mustard and fried onions. Here in Sweden the wayside vendors served their own version – the Swedish 'Korv' – equally tasty and sustaining. When we had covered two hundred and fifty miles we drew off the main road and into a country lane at Kolbach, and settled there for the night.

We awoke to a cloudless sky and the promise of a glorious First of June. A red squirrel was leaping from branch to branch on a tree close to the caravan, and in a near-by copse two Wrynecks were calling. The tape-recorder was immediately brought into play and a reasonably good recording made. After a few minutes one of the birds flew off purposefully to a clump of trees outside a farmhouse a little further along the road. We followed hoping to get a closer view, and arrived just in time to see it disappear into a nesting-box placed high up on one of the trees. We drew closer and waited. Presently a snaky head appeared for a moment at the entrance hole, but it was immediately withdrawn. After a further long wait we decided to play back the recording. The effect was quite dramatic. The Wryneck shot out of the hole like a cork from a bottle, and flew off at top speed to its mate now calling aggressively in the woods a hundred yards away.

We were soon on the road again trundling north hour by hour, the caravan cruising along steadily behind. 'Beware Elk' signs now began to appear on the road-sides, particularly where the road ran between a hillside and a lake. Elk like browsing on aquatic vegetation by lakesides and are a traffic hazard as they cross the road to reach their food supply. In England if you hit a sheep or a fallow deer or a New Forest pony the animal suffers but the driver is not at great risk. In Sweden if you hit an elk the consequences can be disastrous. It stands so high on its gawky legs that the animal's body smashes through the windscreen often with fatal results for all concerned.

A brief stop was made at Harmosand where nesting-boxes had been affixed to the municipal trees in the busy main street. As we sat in the car and tackled our 'Korvs', a male Pied Flycatcher alighted at the entrance to one of the boxes and delivered a full-throated burst of flycatcher song into the interior, presumably at his sitting mate. It must have been a deafening performance at such short range. On we went again, speeding north along the E.4 – mile upon mile of pine and spruce and silver birch, through a landscape sculpted from granite with the bed-rock showing at roadside cuttings – tiny scratch-marks on the Baltic Shield. It was beside one such cutting that we came to a halt after a three hundred and fifty mile long day. We were a few miles from Docksta. Behind us towered a dark, conifer-clad mountainside. Below us lay the Bothnian Gulf, placid in the evening sun. We had a leisurely meal: we strolled about in the warm, still evening air: we stretched and yawned and thought about bed. It was after 11 p.m. but still absurdly light. And then . . . first one chorister . . . and then another . . . and another started tuning up. All at once the air was full of lovely sound. From all sides poured the glorious flute-like notes of Blackbird and Song Thrush, of Redwing and Fieldfare. It was the Vesper Hour. Scores and scores of birds were joining in.

Time passed: midnight was approaching but still the birds sang on. All through the midnight hour the chorus continued in full splendour, and then, as daylight strengthened, it increased in variety and power as a host of other birds began to greet the dawn. Here, in this high latitude away up in the Bothnian Gulf we were, at midnight, in a strange half-world where Vespers and Dawn Chorus overlapped. For the 'Thrush-Blackbird' family – the Turdidae – this darkening and lightening of their world in one consecutive sweep meant a continuous vocal performance – a non-stop midnight matinée – of more than two hours' duration each day and every day at this time of year between dusk and dawn.

Did this, perhaps, account for the astonishing power and quality of the singing in this part of the world? If, for countless generations, the birds of this region, because of their geographical situation, had had their vocal powers unusually extended, might they not in the course of time have developed a special talent for song? A vocal sub-species? It was an intriguing thought. Suffice for us as we lay listening, incredulous, in the Docksta dawn, that each virtuoso performer seemed endowed with quite extraordinary gifts. The magic of the northlands was in each vibrating throat. It is a memory we shall always treasure.

In spite of settling down finally to sleep in the rosy dawn we were up early. We stepped outside the caravan to sniff the morning air. A linnet-like twittering came from the roadside verge, and little puffs of grey smoke seemed to be coming from a patch of dandelions there.

Half a dozen Siskins were industriously scattering dandelion clocks as they quested for seed. And then, from the pinewoods frowning down on our roadside halt came a curious, throaty chuckle as a splendid Black Woodpecker, in a series of mighty aerial bounds, came swooping down the hillside towards the trees by the water's edge. It was our first sight of this magnificent bird, and we never want to have a better. We could have lingered in that delightful spot for hours, but another day of hard travel lay ahead. We had lunch near a cottage in whose garden Pied Flycatchers were busily inspecting nesting-boxes erected on silver birches by the roadside. As we moved into northern Sweden hay-drying racks began to appear in the fields, and, further north still, hay-barns in all the fields. New species of ducks began to show up on these northern lakes. Scaup were identified on more than one occasion.

Near Rana we noticed, high in the sky and travelling on a parallel course, a large grey and white raptor – an Osprey. A couple of miles ahead we could see a great sheet of water. When we reached a causeway that spanned the lake we halted. The Osprey was in a hunting mood. It was circling the lake and losing height, fanning its wings and hovering, and lowering its talons in readiness for a strike. And then, suddenly, came a swift, downward plunge followed by a quick splash, and a mighty flapping of wings as it rose from the water with a fine fish in its talons. Then, after a brief pause in the air – a check in flight to shake out water from its plumage – it rose in mounting spirals to a great height – almost out of range of the unaided eye – and set forth homewards, a steady, purposeful flight due south, back to its eyrie by some distant lake. The young ornithologists we had met in southern Sweden had told us that Ospreys seldom fish their own home waters. It was a very happy chance that brought the Osprey and the three of us together at the lakeside near Rana on that afternoon in early June. An Osprey is always a bird that is well worth watching, and to see one fishing had been a rare privilege.

Between Lulea and Haparanda the temperature dropped surprisingly. We saw our first snow – the remains of winter drifts beside the road. We passed a succession of rivers in full spate, all of them carrying logs to the Gulf. Spring ploughing was just beginning in the turfy fields beside the sea. And so we arrived at Haparanda – 'The Gateway to the North' – at eight o'clock in the evening on the second of June, and a colder, bleaker frontier town it would be hard to imagine. The sun was shining, but an icy wind was blowing down the River Kemi as we drew off the road and on to the riverside wasteland which we took to be the municipal camp and caravan site. It had an air of complete desolation. I think that we were without question the first visitors to use the site this year. We were weary with travel and shivering with the cold. We climbed into the caravan, battened down everything, and let rip with the calor gas. In five minutes the walls and windows were streaming with condensation but we were gloriously snug and warm. Provided the calor gas held out we were ready for the North Pole. But we had to admit that the Haparanda temperature had given us a distinct shock. Here it was still winter. We appeared to be travelling onwards in space and backwards in season.

Our dimensions were getting confused. It was all rather odd, and particularly the brightness of the midnight hour – and the absurdity of going to bed as the sun began to climb the cold, clear northern sky.

11

Into Finnish Lapland

W E SLEPT late and awoke to find that the wind had dropped and the outside temperature was now quite tolerable. We visited the town and bought 'Jungle Oil' – a powerful insect repellant – in readiness for the mosquito menace further north. We laid in further stores, and visited a bookshop where the Eng. Lit. section, in translation, ranged impressively from Enid Blyton to *Fanny Hill*. We passed a travel agent's in whose window, prominently displayed, was the latest poster from my own home town of Brighton – now, at the beginning of June at its freshest and loveliest, with the gardens in the Old Steine and in the Royal Pavilion grounds a blaze of colour. Here the tulips in the municipal square had half-inch shoots just beginning to push through the dry, dusty soil.

At noon we crossed over from Sweden to Finland at the border town of Tornio half a mile away and set forth for Rovaniemi and the Arctic Circle. A Great Grey Shrike perched on telephone wires on the outskirts of Tornio seemed to confirm for us a welcome to Finland that had already been expressed most charmingly by a uniformed young lady at the Customs. We proposed to spend the night at Rovaniemi, eighty miles up in Finnish

Lapland. Just before reaching there we crossed a wonderful marshland area alive with birds. There were Ruffs and Reeves, Wood-Sandpipers and Snipe, and tiny Temminck's Stints that hovered, moth-like, with whir-ring wings above the clumps of cotton grass where they might soon be nesting. Wigeon and Tufted Duck were swimming in the open water, and a Short-eared Owl was quartering the reed beds in search of prey. It was as promising an area as we had come across anywhere in our travels, but a busy road cut across its entire length, and a prolonged exploration would have had to be con-ducted too much in the public eye.

We drew into Rovaniemi and across the River Kemi with its thousands of logs endlessly floating past, and on to the pleasant car and caravan park by the riverside. We visited the town and concluded that prices in Finnish Lapland were fifty per cent up on prices in England. After supper we went northwards for a couple of miles to have the satisfaction of reaching the Arctic Circle before returning to bed. An impressive roadside sign told us in five languages when we were there. A pleasant log cabin provided excellent coffee, and we sent off post-cards stamped with the Arctic Circle postmark. We returned to the caravan at ten o'clock but it was far too light to think of going to bed, so we decided to go back to the marsh for a further hour or two. It was midnight when we returned. The sun was just below the horizon but the sky was bright with the promise of dawn. We took photographs of the caravan in silhouette against the pale green waters of the River Kemi, and, reluctantly we went to bed.

The others slept, but I was far too full of the excite-

A pair of Dotterels on Mt. Aligas,
Finnish Lapland.

7

Red-spotted Bluethroat challenging
a tape-recording of its own song.
Karigasniemi.

Male Bar-tailed Godwit brooding.
Mt. Aligas, Finnish Lapland.

8

A Mealy Redpoll refuses to leave
its newly-hatched young.
Karigasniemi.

ment and restlessness of an Arctic Spring, and I lay watching the colours change on the distant hills and on the nearby water as the sun cleared the horizon and began to climb the sky. Suddenly two small grey and white ducks, flying up river, alighted in a patch of clear water less than twenty yards away. They were Smew – a duck and a drake – and looking incredibly well-groomed in their immaculate spring plumage. After a few moments they scuttered off upstream with a whirr of wings – very Guillemot-like in flight – and were lost to view. It was a pleasant observation with which to round off a happy day – or, more truthfully, with which to start a new one. It was half-past two in the morning, and although it was the middle of the night the sun was high in the sky. People were strolling about outside as though it were midday. I suppose that after a time one becomes adjusted to perpetual daylight, but we were new to it. Our natures still demanded sleep. As I lay down and closed my eyes waves of weariness came surging over me and I went out like a light.

We awoke to find that the Union Jack had been run up on the flagpole on the caravan site in our honour. We made some final purchases in Rovaniemi. The town had a decidedly wintry look. Silver birches were barely in bud. It was a late spring, we were told. The vegetation certainly confirmed this impression. How the birds and wildlife in general would react to the lateness of the season we had yet to find out.

We bought picture postcards of Laps in costume, said our farewells, and headed north. For the next three weeks we should be within the Arctic Circle. Lapland proper was about to begin. A new roadside sign now began to appear – 'Beware Reindeer'. But it was always 'Beware Reindeer' for a specified distance – three, four or five kilometres. The reason for this is that on their seasonal migrations reindeer follow ancestral routes across Lapland, and these are usually on quite a narrow front. It matters not to them that man has, in the last twenty or thirty years, pushed up roads through Lapland along which cars and lorries travel at lethal speeds. The reindeer continue to use the routes along which their ancestors have travelled for thousands of years. In late spring, when the mosquitoes become unbearable in the lowlands, they move up to the hills, and in the autumn they return. During the winter months they browse on 'reindeer moss' – a pale green, rubbery lichen that carpets the forest floor in these parts. With their great hoofs they scrape away the snow to reach this vital food supply. One might suppose that the great depth of snow in Lapland would mean for them a constant danger of starvation. In fact the snowfall is comparatively light. Precipitation, whether of rain or snow, amounts to only twelve inches a year compared with two and a half times that amount in Britain. Snow is not a major hazard. The discomforts of a Lapland winter are brought about by darkness and perpetual cold.

We maintained a vigilant watch for reindeer, and it was not long before a small herd crossing the road brought us to a halt. As they moved into the cover of the trees we followed, hoping for some photographs. Their wide hoofs were far more suited to the squelchy wilderness in which we found ourselves than were our everyday shoes, so we soon desisted and retraced our steps to the car. When we were scarcely fifteen paces from the road a small wader slipped away unobtrusively from a tangle of low-growing herbage and flew off deeper into the wood. There, in a neat mossy cup lay four most beautiful eggs, each one heavily blotched with chocolate and purple on a sea-green ground. They were unlike any wader eggs that we had seen before. They could belong to one bird only – the Wood-Sandpiper – and while we were kneeling by the nest the anxious parent came trotting into view and stood some twenty yards away in the shadowy woodland, piping softly, and clearly most anxious to return.

We quickly erected a low hide screened with fir branches, and I was installed within. In less than five minutes the bird had returned. Not altogether satisfied with my preliminary shots, I flapped the front of the hide and sent her trotting away. She was back in two minutes, and thereafter it became increasingly difficult to move her from the nest. It was not long before we were standing in the open a couple of yards from the nest and taking turns to photograph her as she returned to brood. As a final test of her fearlessness my brother lay down and composed himself as if for sleep with his head pillowed on the moss a foot away from where she would have to return. He closed his eyes and lay quite still. Through the viewfinder of the ciné camera he looked harmless enough. His woolly Norwegian sweater had a pleasantly furry appearance, and a week's growth of beard on his chin blurred his features and gave him something of the appearance of a benevolent reindeer. I had my finger on the push-button of the camera and the motor was fully wound. Presently the courageous little Wood-Sandpiper came edging forward and into my field of vision. I pressed the button and the mechanism began whirring away. Fearlessly she came and stood by the nest, peering forward to inspect the sleeping human. Satisfied that he was intending her no harm she shuffled on to her eggs and sat brooding there. Not until she had finally settled did the ciné motor die. I was highly delighted with her performance. Whatever else Lapland held in store the Wood-Sandpiper was well and truly on the record. But then came a sobering thought. If all Lapland birds were as amenable as this one, and we as susceptible to their charms, we should run out of film long before we reached the Arctic Sea. We ought to take thought for the morrow and be less prodigal in our expense of film. But in spite of these misgivings we went on our way rejoicing, and secretly unrepentant. A wonderful opportunity had come our way and we had grasped it to the full.

We still had a long journey before us if we were to achieve our target for the day, and the roads were becoming rough and unpleasantly corrugated. We were aiming to cover a hundred and forty miles in the hope of reaching Vuotso where we proposed to turn off eastwards towards the marshlands of Mutenia not many miles from the Russian border. Again we were taking our cue from Alan Davidson who had investigated this area several years ago and written enthusiastically of its richness of bird life. Before reaching Vuotso we stopped for a half-hour's respite from travel and a brew-up of tea. It gave us an opportunity to hear a new song – that of the Brambling. We were entering the kingdom of these northern finches. From now onwards and until we reached the Arctic Sea we should seldom be out of range of the wheezy, grittling repetitive notes of these birds. The song is an unattractive blend of Corn Bunting and Greenfinch notes. The 'bree…ee…eeze' call of a Greenfinch particularly came to mind, but the monotony of the Corn Bunting's song was there, and its association with telephone wires and barbed-wire fences. The real music of Lapland comes from wild wader cries in the marshes, and from Redwings and Bluethroats in the woodlands, and from gallant little Willow Warblers that have struggled up here all the way from North Africa, and are as plentiful in the birches along a Lapland road as they are in the trees along an English country lane. A new wagtail was now encountered – the Grey-headed Wagtail, a north Scandinavian version of the Blue-headed Wagtail we had met in the Low Countries, and a variant of the Yellow Wagtail that we see in English water meadows.

While we were having tea we were startled by a large piebald animal that came lolloping out of the wood and across the road. Predominantly grey, it had startlingly black ear tips and a white tail, and there were large white patches on its body. It was an Arctic Hare in partial moult, and three other hares similarly clad appeared in hot pursuit. It was March madness in early June, and the Lapland version was all the more amusing because the jesters all wore motley, and no two were dressed alike.

We turned off the highway at Vuotso and went rumbling down the bumpy gravel road towards Mutenia. It was getting late and we were glad to draw off into a woodland clearing when we were fairly near to the marshes that we hoped to explore on the morrow. We had supper to the accompaniment of Redwing and Brambling song, and, tempting though it was to linger out of doors in the bright light of approaching midnight, we needed sleep and went to bed.

After an early breakfast we set off to explore the marsh. Within fifty yards of entering that wonderful wilderness of tussocky bogland we found ourselves floundering about in the morass. But it was not quite as alarming as it seemed. You sank for a certain distance, perhaps two feet or more, and then came to solid footing, not of rock or gravel, but of ice. No doubt as the season advanced the depth of bog would increase, but it was comforting to realize that we were now in the region of permafrost. Always below a certain depth the ground would be frozen solid.

But there were drier ridges that we could follow if we took time to discover them. They went weaving about the marsh in crazy patterns, but being above the water level they were likely nesting places for the marshland birds. It was not long before a wader the size of a Redshank but lacking its crescent wing-bars slipped off her nest. As she alighted we had little difficulty in identifying her as a Reeve. The nest had four eggs and the bird was sitting hard. In one particularly watery area of the marsh was a little rushy island where a dozen Ruffs were displaying continually with great vigour. A splendid tourney was in progress, and it was interesting to see that Ruffs were in the same stage of their breeding-cycle here in Lapland in early June as they had been in the Netherlands a full month earlier. Wood-Sandpipers were 'tinkling', and a pair of Spotted Redshanks came winging across the marsh with loud 'chewit...chewit' cries from the edge of some adjacent woodland. They, too, would be nesting by now, but unless we stumbled across the nest by accident it would require a good deal of patient watching to track them down.

As we moved forward across our first Lapland bog we were surprised to find ant-hills seething with life on the drier ridges. Lizards kept scuttling for cover just ahead of us, and frogs were spawning in shallow pools. I recollected finding frog-spawn in my garden pool in Sussex a fortnight before leaving England in mid-April. Here they were about to start their breeding-cycle in the first week of June.

After an hour's exploration we returned to the waiting car, and it was then, from high up in the air above the marsh, there came to our ears that unearthly sound we had heard at Varnamo just over a week before. Hollow hoof-beats were sounding in the sky – 'lok–toggi... lok–toggi...lok–toggi...lok–toggi'. A phantom horseman was riding by. We were in Jack Snipe country again.

As we returned to the main road at Vuotso to resume our journey north we passed scattered villages where House Martins were building their mud nests under the eaves of Lap cottages, and where Lap housewives wearing their traditional headdress waved to us as we went by.

Between Vuotso and Ivalo we had a lunch stop by a little stream spanned by a narrow bridge. The ground was pitted with bomb craters now brimming with water in which toads were spawning. Shell cases and fragments of twisted metal littered the ground. It seemed extraordinary that an inoffensive little bridge like this could have attracted so much violence some twenty-five years ago when the Germans were pulling out. A few silver birches had sprung up, and a soft mantle of moss

151

now covered the scars of war. From one of the birches there suddenly burst forth a snatch of glorious song – a powerful and astonishing volley of notes that came from a bird about the size of a Robin. There was, too, something Robin-like about its form and the way it took its stance. But its throat, instead of being a rusty orange-red, was a startling, heavenly blue above a chestnut fringe – but the blue was not entire, for in its centre was a tell-tale vivid spot – a splash of brilliant red. This was the Bluethroat in its red-spotted Scandinavian form – the lovely 'Lapland Robin'. And how that little bird could sing! With quivering body and palpitating throat it poured forth a torrent of sparkling notes – a cascade of glittering sound – and then, down it came, planing on outstretched wings to the level ground, and continued to sing ecstatically there as it moved about, filled with an urgent restlessness, among the mossy stones. Its song was a cry of rapture: it was the very ecstasy of spring.

Reluctantly we left this charmed spot and journeyed on, through Ivalo and past Lake Inari, still covered with black ice but with watery edges showing in which Mergansers were swimming, and Smew and Velvet Scoters, Pintail and Goldeneye, and a pair of Black-throated Divers in a setting of blue water and the sombre green of distant pines. It was colder up here. Snow was heaped in drifts by the roadsides. Spruces and pines were thinning out and birches were increasing. It was getting too cold for the conifers: we were nearing the birch zone. The croaking of Ravens was now a recurring sound. From time to time, on stretches of treeless, open country, high slatted snow-fences lined the gravelled roads and somewhat impeded the view.

Reindeer were frequently encountered, many of them on the move. We were heading for the environs of Karigasniemi and a roadside quarry where, a year before, my friend John Reynolds had pitched his little tent. A map that he had sent us gave a wealth of local detail. With any luck, he had said, we should find the actual site. Arctic Ringed Plovers should be nesting on the gravels by the roadside. There were Bluethroats in the copse hard by, and a stream would give us all the water we should need. And, as for food supplies, the store in the little Lap township a few miles away would furnish all our needs – but don't forget to take your own baked beans, was John's advice. The Laps have yet to discover the incomparable benefits conferred on mankind by the firm of Heinz.

And so, at 10 p.m., in broad daylight, we neared another Promised Land. We slowed down when the quarry came in sight and took our bearings. Immediately, from the roadside gravels, came the plaintive piping of a Ringed Plover disturbed at its nest. A volley of welcoming Bluethroat song sounded from the birches near at hand. We drew the car off the road and brought it to a halt beside a drift of snow that reached half-way up the caravan windows. Stiff with travel we staggered out and went for a brief look round. There, fifty yards away and chuckling cheerfully to itself, was the promised stream. There, too, concealed in an empty oil drum abandoned by the road menders, were a few rusty tins. We picked one up and examined the label. Even after a year's exposure to the elements it told us all we needed to know. Good old John! Good old baked beans! We had hit the exact spot.

12

Bird Life in the Birch Zone

OUR week in the environs of Karigasniemi began
auspiciously. We awoke to the sparkle of sun on
snow and the promise of a glorious day, and it was not
long before our rucksacks were packed and we were
setting forth along the road to Karigasniemi. By the
side of the road a short distance away we found a small,
secluded lake enclosed by steep, birch-covered banks still
mantled in snow. Patches of ice were drifting on its surface, but swimming amongst them and darting here and
there as they snatched up food from the surface were a
score of dainty waders, buoyant as corks, and delight-
fully unafraid. We scrambled down the bank to the
water's edge to watch our first Red-necked Phalaropes.
The nearest were now a dozen yards away. While we
moved into position they simply sat still on the water
and watched us: as soon as we halted they started
moving – not away from us but just continuing their
active, jerky pursuit of mosquito larvae in the pool.
Gradually they moved closer, the sun shining on their
russet backs and bringing out the lovely, glowing colour
of their rufous bibs. Nearer and nearer they swam until
they were only three or four feet away and seemingly
quite oblivious of our presence. They were swimming in

pairs and occasional display was taking place. A little Phalarope cock would fly at his mate, hover over her momentarily and alight on her back as she swam in the water, but mostly they were engrossed in their quest for food. We watched them for a long time. It was difficult to tear ourselves away, but other delights were awaiting us a little lower down the pool. Here the ice was more uniformly spread, but there were patches of open water and on one of these two extraordinary-looking ducks were swimming. The drake had a long black streamer trailing behind for half his length. They were Long-tailed Ducks, and when they took to the air six Goldeneyes leapt up to join them. We climbed back on to the road and continued on our way, but every few yards a new sight or sound called for a halt and a fuller investigation. Sailing overhead and mewing softly as it flew was our first Rough-legged Buzzard. Perched on a tree on the skyline was another raptor, a small falcon with hunched-up wings. It dashed off at our approach and revealed its identity – a Merlin.

We were soon to discover, too, that here in the Karigasniemi woods we would seldom be out of the range of Bluethroat song. Everywhere this little Lapland Robin, like his cousin in a gentler English setting, was making vocal declaration of his territorial rights. Willow Warblers were similarly employed, and, from the quality and volume of Redwing and Brambling song to be heard on every side, it was apparent that we had arrived in northern Lapland, at the end of the first week in June, exactly at the right time. A fortnight ago Lapland was scarcely emerging from the icy grip of winter. A fortnight hence and summer would be here. Our timing had been perfect. In spite of ice and snowdrifts we were right in the heart of spring. Again and again we caught sight of a bird with moss, or hay, or feather in its bill. A million homes were in the making: the nesting season had begun.

And there were others on the Karigasniemi road who shared our good fortune. Striding towards us with binoculars at the ready and with rucksacks on their backs came the personification of adventurous youth – two cheerful, healthy-looking types, one a tall, rangy, young fellow with a straggling beard, the other a lithe, suntanned girl. We exchanged greetings and discovered that they came from the Netherlands. They were on a four-months' hitch-hiking and bird-watching adventure. Everything that they needed they carried on their backs. They had worked up the coast of Norway, visited the Lofoten Islands, and made their way round the northern coastline in temperatures and under climatic conditions that must have been, at times, absolutely appalling. They were now making for a Lap hut, one of a chain set up by the Finnish Youth Service along a trail across this part of Lapland. There they hoped to enjoy rather more comfort and certainly warmer conditions than they had experienced for many a week past in the small light-weight tent they normally used. They spoke English in a simple way that was entirely adequate for normal conversational purposes. It required only a little practice for them to become really fluent: and this practice was soon forthcoming. As a result of this chance encounter on the Karigasniemi road we struck up such a happy friendship with them that we joined forces, and had the pleasure of

their company for the next two weeks – an arrangement
that, for our part, was to be to our inestimable benefit.
It was Anneke's first visit to Lapland, but Henk had
been here before. He knew what to look for and where
it might be found. He was steeped in Lap lore and Lapland 'know-how'. His knowledge of the birds and wildlife
of the region was profound, and he was generosity itself
in his eagerness to share it with newcomers like ourselves. Moreover he had a delightful sense of humour
and was never out of sorts: he was, in fact, an ideal
companion on a venture such as this. And what of
Anneke? I think that if the truth be told we had all lost
our hearts to her by the end of the fortnight – just a little.
It was understandable. To see a girl like Anneke striding
along a road in the heart of Lapland on a June day was a
small miracle in itself. But when we found that this same
girl, scorning all offers of aid, could leap a stream, or
climb a tree, or find on a mountain scree a nest that had
escaped all other eyes – then our admiration knew no
bounds. And, too, there was her welcome presence at
our evening meals. The ritual of after-dinner coffee in
china cups was now observed, and the table linen, alas by
now far from fresh, responded somehow to the feminine
touch. It is Woman, without question, who is the real
civilizer of the human race. Man invents gadgets, all
bristling with masculinity, for ease of living in the open
– tin-openers and sheath-knives, enamel plates and mugs,
and three-in-one cutlery sets. With tools like these he
has the basic equipment for eating, but there is more to a
civilized meal than the ability to demolish it with
weapons of one sort or another. So far we had not slipped
very far from grace at meal-times – except, perhaps, in

the matter of washing-up, and the state of our tea-towels. But Anneke's presence helped a great deal. She brought back a touch of graciousness into our living, and we even had flowers on the caravan table. 'Karigas-niemi King Kups' were just coming into bloom by the edge of the nearby stream.

Anneke had been to England as an 'au pair' girl. She had used the time well, and had read widely. I was often surprised by the way she could pick up an allusion. When we called her 'our Wendy', she smiled and said she had enjoyed *Peter Pan*; and a reference to 'No time to stand and stare' had her asking eagerly about *The Auto-biography of a Super Tramp* which she wanted very much to read. I suspect that she and W. H. Davies would have had a lot in common.

Our first expedition together took place within an hour of our meeting. Henk had a mind to search for Dotterels on Mount Aligas, a high hill still mostly snow-covered that overlooked a rising valley within easy walking distance of our base. At the head of the valley was a reindeer corral and autumn slaughter-ground that John Reynolds had indicated on his map. We could, he said, drive the car up a bumpy track for a mile or more and so cut down walking time on expeditions there. We took him at his word and sallied forth. Before we had gone thirty yards we were axle-deep in snow and slush and had to abandon all hope of progress by mechanical means. So we left the car and proceeded on foot. We soon left the track and worked through the woods where the snow was less impeding. A Redwing's nest neatly perched on a fallen birch was our first discovery, and already it contained four lovely sky-blue eggs. A Brambling's nest also with a full clutch was next discovered some fifteen feet up a slender birch.

When we left the shelter of the woods and began to cross more open country the snow cover thickened. We were soon floundering up to our knees in heavy drifts or breaking through the melting crust into icy water below. Several rushing torrents had to be crossed, but by now we were past caring about trying to keep dry, and we waded happily on. The sun was shining and the day was warm, and all Lapland lay before us waiting to be explored. As we neared the reindeer corral a fearful stench assailed our nostrils. This was the autumn slaughter-ground, and offal from the slaughtered beasts, hidden until recently by the winter snows, was plentifully strewn around. Half a dozen Ravens flew away with reproachful, guttural croaks as we drew near. For them the melting snow would, day by day, disclose some new and appetizing dish. But it was not a pretty sight for human eyes, nor was it a place in which to linger. We stayed only long enough to pick up several fine antlers and a hand-sewn slipper, no doubt lost in a snow-drift by some unhappy Lap.

Although the snow still lay deep in the valley, the wind-swept slopes of the hill towards which we were now trudging were only partially covered. It seemed likely that birds which in a normal spring would nest in the valley bottom would this year be forced to seek the higher slopes. As we neared the hillside we found that birds were reappearing. A Long-tailed Skua flew over, and a pair of Spotted Redshanks came yelping past. Somewhere in the distance a Whimbrel was tittering, and the piping of Northern Golden Plovers was always in our ears.

When we were about two-thirds up the hillside Henk called a halt and summoned a council of war. If Dotterels were here at all, he declared, they would be somewhere along the southern slopes. We should therefore work along the contour line and not climb any higher. I was inclined to disagree for I had always considered the Dotterel to be a bird of the mountain-tops, and to the top of this Lapland hill I was determined to go. So Tim and I left the main party and struggled to the top. For half an hour we searched that bare and stony wilderness on the roof of Lapland without success. We saw a pair of Snow Buntings but nothing else, and so descended to join the others. They were beaming with pleasure. They had walked up to two pairs of Dotterels and had approached to within a dozen yards of them. Satisfactory photographs had been taken before the birds had flown away. Filled with chagrin I had to admit that Henk's instinct for finding birds in the right place was a good deal more reliable than mine. My disappointment was acute, but Henk was optimistic: we should probably find another pair before very long. Ten minutes later we heard a soft piping just ahead of us, and there, miraculously camouflaged against the greys and browns of the hillside, were our Dotterels. The first sight of any new species is always a memorable experience. This long spring journey had already furnished us with many cherished 'firsts', but of all the birds seen the Dotterel now held – and would continue to hold – pride of place. For one thing the setting was superb.

From this lofty elevation the whole of Lapland lay

160

spread out at our feet. Snow-streaked hillocks and hollows extended, fold upon fold, as far as the eye could see. In the valleys the insubstantial birches were blue-grey shadows on a blanket of white. But in the foreground, where the Dotterels had taken their stand, the rocks were lichen-covered, grey and gold, and the stunted herbage russet brown. Against any other background the deep orange of the Dotterels' breasts would have been a sad betrayal. But as we saw them now the deception was complete. For as long as they stood still they were invisible. Let the eye stray from these motionless figures but for a moment and they were gone, and it required quite an effort to will them back again. We were, however, a little too near for their comfort, and as I fumbled with my camera they suddenly took fright and flew away up the hillside and out of sight. But I was not yet ready to admit defeat. While the others began the descent to the valley my brother and I set forth uphill in the general direction of the Dotterels' flight. There might be another plateau up there where they had come to rest. We approached with caution, and eventually came out on a ridge similar in character to the one we had left below. Very slowly, step by step, we advanced. The plaintive piping began again, and we scanned the rocky terrain until our eyes ached, but at last we saw them fifty yards ahead. Cameras in readiness we began our stalk – not a frontal approach but an oblique one, with frequent pauses to let the birds gain confidence. Gradually the distance lessened, and still the Dotterels held their ground. They seemed less inclined to fly this time, and during our pauses they began to move about with apparent unconcern. Nearer and nearer we crept, and soon the cameras were clicking. In the end we had them standing less than ten paces away, and it was only when we had used all the film that we could justifiably expend, even on this exceptional subject, that they decided they had put up with our intrusion long enough. For a moment they stood with wings upraised, and then away they went round a shoulder of the hillside and were lost to view.

Our descent to the valley was a rollicking downhill scramble over boulders and scree, and through snow-drifts into which at times we plunged waist deep. We were glowing with delight: we had had our rendezvous with the Dotterels: another Lapland ambition had been fulfilled.

This success most certainly called for a celebration. Baked beans would not be on the menu tonight. We had a treasured tin of ham, and a wide variety of mildly exotic tinned vegetables culled from shops in various countries through which we had passed, and saved for an occasion such as this. A fruit-jelly was already congeal-ing satisfactorily in our snow-drift 'frig', conveniently sited a few paces from the caravan door. Anneke and Henk joined us round the festive board, and we feasted and chattered away happily until midnight approached; and then, reinvigorated, we climbed a nearby hillock to see the midnight sun. There it was, a great orange ball, well clear of the horizon and about to begin its twelve-hour climb up the northern sky. I lingered there on the hill-top long after the others had returned. I found it very difficult to tear myself away from the strange beauty of the arctic midnight hour. And then, as if this day of days had not bestowed riches enough, there came a final gift. Against the primrose sky a huge grey owl came winnowing past. I could hardly believe my eyes, for never had I seen an owl of such impressive size. Like a great grey ghost it floated by on silent wings. But what on earth could it be? I hastened down to the caravan and tumbled out the bird books there. There was only one bird that fitted the description – the Great Grey or Lapland Owl. We were well within its breeding-range, but it was more a bird of pine forests than of the birch zone. I was puzzled to know where it could be breeding, but two days later we found a possible answer. Less than twenty minutes' flight away was the Tana valley, and on its sloping sides an ancient conifer forest that would provide all the green gloom that a Lapland Owl could possibly require.

The following morning, under a cloudless sky, we set out with Henk and Anneke for an exploration of the vast, marshy wilderness that extended as far as the eye could see westwards from our base. Not all the terrain was marsh. In between the boglands were hummocky knolls and hillocks covered with sparse birch trees. For the discerning eye the landscape offered a striking example of the after-effects of glaciation, and Tim, our geographer and geologist, was full of enthusiastic appreciation. Here and there we kept coming across 'kettle-holes' – sudden, unexpected cavities and depressions where, in post-glacial times great solid lumps of ice had melted and left their tell-tale hollows. We had lunch on a classic example of glacial deposition – a gravelly drumlin. The day was hot and windless with temperatures nearing the seventies. Snow was melting fast, and the low-lying areas were swilling with water. Phalaropes were 'spinning' for mosquito larvae on the numerous pools, but appeared not yet to be breeding. A Willow Grouse sprang from its place of concealment in the dense undergrowth. It flew off 'go-backing' hoarsely with much the same cautionary tone of voice as the Red Grouse, its British counterpart, on a Scottish moor. Wherever birches appeared on the drumlins and glacial gravels, Bluethroats were singing. On all sides Redwings were gorging on the ripe northern bilberries that the melting snow hourly disclosed. A prodigious banquet awaits these hungry thrushes on their arrival in Lapland from their winter quarters in the south. At the end of the brief arctic summer the berry crop is barely ripening by the time the birds begin their passage south. Blanketed by the winter snows, this store of fruit remains in deep-freeze for the next eight months. With the thaw in late May and early June the berries see the light of day again – but not for long. The Redwings see to that. Out of curiosity I sampled the berries. The sugar content was rather low, but in spite of a certain astringency they were quite acceptable to the human palate. It was at least comforting to know that if one were unfortunate or incompetent enough to get lost for a day or two in a Lapland bog at this time of year there would be no need to starve.

The northern-nesting waders were here again, but the area was so vast that the discovery of a nest would be more a matter of chance than design. Spotted Redshanks, Whimbrels and Golden Plovers were all giving their distinctive calls, and we watched a pair of Greenshanks gloriously display-flighting against a backcloth of clear blue sky. Again we heard those hollow hoof-beats clopping overhead – there were Jack Snipes breeding here. And then, from somewhere high overhead, a Raven urgently croaked. 'Always look up when a Raven croaks,' said Henk. 'There will be a good reason.' And up there a pair of Golden Eagles and a Rough-legged Buzzard went sailing by. The Raven was in hot pursuit. He was showing these raptors off the premises, but it was a mere gesture of defiance on his part. Unperturbed, they sailed majestically on their way.

Bumble bees with furry golden behinds tapering to a bright yellow were buzzing about in search of early-flowering sallows. Our first Lapland butterfly flew past. It had dark brown forewings with prominent eye-spots, and orange under-wings. Two pairs of wild geese flew past at a distance as we began our journey home. They were probably Bean Geese but we could not be certain. We returned to the caravan in the late afternoon. We had not covered many miles but the going had been heavy and the day unexpectedly hot. We were more than ready for supper and an early bed.

A Bluethroat singing in the birches just outside the caravan awakened me the following morning, and its volley of song reminded me that the tape-recorder had not yet come into use during our stay in Kargasniemi. To return from Lapland without a recording of Blue-throat song would be unthinkable. It was comparatively easy to stalk this ardent songster, for in its assertion of its territorial rights the Bluethroat seems oblivious of all else but the virtuosity of its own performance. Having obtained what I considered must be more than a satis-factory recording, I retired a few yards and tried a 'play-back', forgetting for the moment the possible effect that this might have on the performer. No sooner did the Bluethroat hear its own challenging song coming from the tape-recorder than it came whizzing towards me like a winged bullet, only checking its aggressive flight just in time to avoid a head-on collision with the strange metal box resting on my knee. I switched off the recording and paused to consider how best to profit from this intriguing discovery. Somehow I must get a photographic record – but how? First, a suitable site must be found. The base of a birch tree that forked a few inches above ground level was chosen. The tape-recorder could stand on the ground, and the aggressive little bird might then come hopping through the fork in search of it. The camera was mounted on its tripod and carefully focused. In the view-finder the top half of the tape-recorder could just be seen: above it was the forked branch. All was in readiness. I switched on, and quickly stepped back behind the camera. I was only just in time. In a flash the Bluethroat whizzed across the intervening space and came bustling through the fork of the tree to perch for an instant an inch or two away from the mysterious box from which its song was now outpouring. I just had time to press the shutter lever before this volatile creature, whose reactions were ten times faster than mine, went speeding off. It had come to an instant decision that it was being fooled. Several times I tried again but could get no further reaction. It was a clear case of 'Once bitten, twice shy'. That little Bluethroat had learnt its lesson with astonishing speed. There might be other Bluethroats elsewhere who would fall for that particular trick – but not he!

Later that morning we went into Karigasniemi to post

letters and renew our stores. Lapland was experiencing its first heat-wave of the year. Temperatures were well up in the seventies, and Lap children were running about in improvised sun-suits. The little township consisted of about three dozen houses, a Post Office, two General Stores, a builder's yard and garage, and a 'Baari' complete with jukebox and the latest 'Top of the Pops'. The teenagers of Karigasniemi had caught the current craze. It was springtime in Lapland: flowers had appeared on the earth: the time of the singing birds had come: and the voice of the Beatles was heard in the land! So much, we thought, for travelling to the Land of the Midnight Sun to get away from it all.

We soon left the town and went to explore the eastern bank of the River Tana where pine woods surprisingly clothed the steep slopes. We hoped to see Grosbeaks and Waxwings, but we had no success and soon returned to our happier hunting-grounds in the Aligas region. I wanted to return to the Dotterel hill-slopes with the ciné camera, and Henk was more than ready to accompany me. The others were more inclined to spend the afternoon in camp, with a bathe in the stream in prospect. The day was now oppressively hot and we were all feeling its effects. Henk and I set forth heavily laden, and were soon toiling up the slopes and into refreshingly cooler air. We searched an hour for the Dotterels but without success. However, we found a Snow Bunting nest-site, and watched the hen – with the cock in solicitous attendance – tugging at dead grass stems from the edges of snow drifts, and flying off with them to her nest in a pile of boulders. Eventually, compelled to admit defeat over the Dotterels, we began our descent to the valley below. Half-way down we came out on to a stony plateau sparsely clothed with tundra vegetation – mosses and lichens, and stunted grass and scrub.

We were walking about thirty yards apart when suddenly Henk halted and pointed to the sky. Coming down the valley towards us, but at a considerable height, was a huge white owl that glided majestically on its way, occasionally fanning its great, rounded wings. The Lapland Owl I had seen a few hours before was impressive enough, but this vast white bird now floating overhead and magnificently outlined against the blue sky was in a class by itself. There was, in fact, only one bird that it could possibly be, and Henk immediately confirmed my own diagnosis. In a voice that pealed out like a trumpet-call over the stony wastes he yelled: 'Snowy Owl!' As he did so a most remarkable thing happened. Almost from under his feet – with startling suddenness – a bird exploded into the air, rocketing away and yelping for all it was worth. Henk looked down eagerly, and then, straightening himself up to his full six foot three, made ready for utterance. This was his great moment. He was no longer Henk, a Dutch boy foot-loose in Lapland. He was the Great Explorer who has sighted his goal: he was Columbus making his landfall: he was Cortés gazing at the Pacific. In clear, ringing, authoritative tones he announced, not only to me but to all Lapland and to his fellow ornithologists in the far-away Netherlands: 'I have found a Bar-tailed Godwit's nest!'

It was an incredible stroke of luck. If the Snowy Owl had not flown over at that precise moment, and if Henk had not halted and shouted to me, the Bar-tailed Godwit would have continued to crouch unobserved. Her camouflage was such that we could have passed within a couple of feet and still not have seen her there. We almost executed a war-dance on the spot. Not only for Henk, but for us all, the finding of a Bar-tailed Godwit's nest on this trip had been one of the ultimate ambitions. All the way from the Camargue we had had this bird in our sights. Its own migratory journey was, in a very real sense, synonymous with ours. At the end of April Godwits were already mustering on the saline étangs of the Rhône delta when we were there. We had watched them on the mud flats of the Yser estuary in Belgium a week later. We had successfully lain in wait for them as they massed on the edge of the tide north of the Schorren on Texel in mid-May. We had seen them on the saltings of the Limfjord in northern Denmark a week later. And now we were gazing down at a Bar-tailed Godwit's nest on the slopes of Mount Aligas in northern Lapland. It was a gift from the gods, unsought and undeserved, and presented to us in the strangest of ways — with the compliments of a passing Snowy Owl. What a fantastic place is Lapland! The discovery, too, was all the sweeter for the knowledge that although there might be thousands of Godwits breeding in northern Lapland, the finding of a nest could still be a matter of pure chance.

I think it was this discovery that determined, more than anything else, the pattern of our activities in Karigasniemi during the few days that remained to us there. As soon as it was practicable, Henk and I were determined on attempting a stalk of the sitting bird. We returned to base in great jubilation and with keen anticipation of what the morrow might hold in store.

After supper and just before midnight a solitary Waxwing was sighted in the birch trees just beyond the stream. Henk, who was camping in that direction, was whistled up. He came scrambling out of his tent in his pyjamas. On seeing the bird he dived back for his camera with its enormous telephoto lens, emerged again, and went off in cautious pursuit. I went to bed reflecting that there could be very few places in the world where you would see an enthusiast in pyjamas, camera in hand, stalking a bird through the woods by the light of the Midnight Sun.

With a startling suddenness the temperature dropped in the night, and the following morning there were flurries of snow falling from a seemingly clear sky. A great influx of Sand Martins had occurred while we were asleep, and dozens were now hawking over the Phalarope pool which we passed on our way along the now familiar road to Aligas. In the birch woods we found our first Mealy Redpoll's nest, and another Brambling's with a full clutch before we started our ascent to the Godwit plateau.

We prepared ourselves for a really cautious approach, and were still two hundred yards away when we moved into single file and began stealthily moving forward. This caution not only reaped its own reward but also yielded a handsome bonus. Another bird whose presence on this plateau was so far unsuspected suddenly rose from its nest and flew off with 'tittering' cries. It was a Whimbrel, the lesser Curlew of the northern moors. We noted the approximate point of its departure and continued our approach. Through the binoculars at fifty yards we could just make out the form of the sitting

Godwit. Today it was the male who was crouching on the nest. His rufous plumage made him more conspicuous than his mate of yesterday's encounter. Cautiously, yard by yard, we drew nearer. As soon as his image appeared, even distantly, on the focusing screen I took the first spin of film. Then nearer still, and the camera whirred again. Still nearer – ten yards . . . eight yards . . . six yards . . . his image now completely filled the screen. My still camera was also slung round my neck, so I switched over from one apparatus to the other. The other members of the party crept up behind me and clicked their cameras too. A dozen photographs were taken in about as many seconds, and then – whoosh! – with a flash of white from its underparts that lovely, russet Godwit leapt into the air and fled with 'oiker... oiker...oiker...oiker...' cries, only to alight some fifty yards away, where it continued to abuse us as we stood over its nest. Tim slipped back to scan the area from which the Whimbrel had taken flight, and soon found the nest with its full clutch of eggs. It was a mere forty yards from the Godwit site. Was there an amicable arrangement between the two species, as seems to be the case with Lapwings and Redshanks in an English water meadow?

The successful Godwit stalk had made our day, but a further triumph was in store when, a little later, Anneke found a Northern Golden Plover's nest with two darkly-mottled eggs half a mile further up the hillside.

After lunch we put up a small hide some ten yards from the Godwit's nest in the hope of taking some teleshots of the bird returning. I was installed in the hide and the others withdrew. The Whimbrels, nesting some forty yards away, returned almost at once, and some distant shots were taken of both birds at the nest. The Godwits, however, were not inclined to show themselves, so after half an hour we dismantled the hide and gave up the attempt.

On our way back to the road we found a Bluethroat's nest almost ready for eggs, and a Redwing's with six eggs ideally sited for photography. We put up the basic structure of a hide and promised ourselves some entertainment there the following day. After tea we spent a happy hour filming and photographing at the Phalarope pool. Tim went off on a lone prowl in the woods. He returned a couple of hours later with wide eyes and a startled look. In the birch woods by the edge of the great marsh he had encountered a wolf! Fortunately for his self-respect the wolf had bolted first. But this was a new aspect of wildlife in Karigasniemi that added spice to our explorations there. After this we kept a sharp look-out, particularly for footprints, and we found spoor on more than one occasion, but the author of the tracks was not glimpsed again. We were also sampling the small mammal population hereabouts with Longworth traps in which these small creatures are put to the inconvenience of temporary captivity before release. We were hoping for Lemmings but succeeded only in catching several lively specimens of the Ruddy Vole – charming little animals with a decidedly rusty hue to their glossy fur.

A late evening stroll up the course of the stream yielded another Redwing's nest with a clutch of seven, and a second Redpoll's in the cleft of a fallen birch. The sitting bird was determined not to leave, and we filmed

172

her openly at very short range, and even stroked her tail. From a thicket of birches near the source of the stream came a scrambling of birds disturbed from a roost. When they had cleared the trees and were in full view we counted no less than forty Ravens in the air at the same time. We inspected the roost. The birches were all heavily 'whitewashed' and the odour distinctly strong. We only stayed long enough to collect a bunch of fine, black quills from the scores that were lying around. Although it was two hours before midnight, the light was little different in strength and quality from that of the midday hours, but all the birds of this region seemed to sense that this was the time for rest. For an hour or two on either side of the bright midnight they quietened down both in activity and song.

That evening another caravan with 'G.B.' plates drew off the road and on to our site. Three elderly adventurers disembarked and came over to make our acquaintance. They hailed from the south-west, and it was pleasant to hear again the soft burr of the Dorset–Hampshire coast. Their real names we never properly discovered until they were about to depart, but we always referred to the two men in the party as Ralph and John. Ralph's was a 'Country Questions' voice: he had the Wightman drawl. To listen to his slow, west-country speech was to hear again the sleepy sounds of life on a Dorset farm. And to listen to John was to hear again the click of leather on willow on an English village green: his was the Arlott voice. They had come to Lapland for the fun of birds-nesting, and, we were later to suspect, for a little egg-collecting too, though not in any serious vein. I

think it was Ralph who was the snapper-up of uncon-
sidered trifles. I suppose it was a form of souvenir-
hunting. There was no mention at any time of any such
thing, but if it were not so, why should he talk of
immersing a clutch of Phalarope's eggs to see if they
were hard-set? Or why should a Lapland Bunting's nest
we found together have four eggs one day and only three
the next?

They joined us the following morning as we set forth
for the Aligas woods and hillside. The Redwing proved
an easy photographic subject, but the Bar-tailed Godwit
was nervous and the Whimbrel also disinclined to return
during a brief period that we spent in concealment nearby. The wind was now so cold again that we feared to
chill the eggs by staying too long in the vicinity. The
only new discovery was a Bluethroat's nest with two
olive-green eggs similar to but somewhat paler than a
Nightingale's.

The following day, June 11th, would be our last in
Karigasniemi. The Arctic Sea was calling. A last assault
by two of us up Aligas again produced no Dotterel, but
Ptarmigan were stalked on a snow-field near the summit,
and distant shots of Northern Golden Plover were taken
before a snow storm compelled us to retire. These were
not soft and fluffy snowflakes, but small, hard sago balls
that were hurled at our faces by the cruel wind. We
gasped with discomfort, and were glad to seek the
shelter of the woods.

Back in camp we found that the others had been
amusing themselves in persuading the little Mealy Redpoll to become hand-tame. She now had newly-hatched
young whom she was determined not to leave. Rather

than be parted from them she would perch on fingers that lifted her gently from the nest. Four more Bramblings' nests were found within a quarter of a mile of our camp, and a similar number of Redwings', one of which, at ground level, we earmarked for further attention on our return.

13

The Arctic Sea Coast

IT WAS now the twelfth of June, and time for us to
head north again and make for the Arctic Sea – and
Henk and Anneke said they would come with us, which
was splendid. But we were scarcely two miles on the
road when disaster struck. Water from the recent thaw
had undermined a portion of the road and caused it to
subside. We hit the cavity with a horrible crunch; the
caravan lurched dangerously to one side, and we came to
a halt in the certain knowledge that something was now
seriously amiss. We had sheared a bolt from the strut
on the caravan undercarriage, and with the strut now
hanging down, the wheel was rubbing furiously on the
caravan casing. An ominous smell of scorching rubber
assailed our nostrils. It was only later, when we found
charred paper on a packet of biscuits in the food locker
adjacent to the friction spot, that we realized how
perilously near we had been to a fire in the caravan itself.
After an hour's toil and a good deal of shoving and
grunting from underneath the caravan, we jacked the
metal bar back into place, and fixed it with a bolt that
we were fortunate to have with us in our box of sundry
spares. With rather more caution we proceeded on
our way.

Emergency repairs to the caravan.
Karigasniemi.

9

We barter with Norwegian fishermen for salmon caught in the Tana River. Norwegian Lapland.

Saltjern, a fishing village on
Varanger Fjord, with a flock of
Steller's Eiders on the weed-strewn
rocks.

10

Arctic Ringed Plover at nest.
Varanger Fjord.

Just beyond Karigasniemi we passed the frontier post and entered Norwegian Lapland. Frontier formalities were negligible. A little girl came trotting out from the Customs House, raised the barrier separating the two countries, and waved us through. Father, we presumed, was otherwise engaged. Salmon were running well in the nearby Tana River. No doubt he had urgent business that had taken him there.

As soon as we entered Norwegian Lapland we noted a more purposeful air, and greater activity in the scattered farmsteads along the road. We even saw an occasional cow. The little Lap town of Karajok had a modern self-service store where we picked up our wire baskets and jostled with Lap housewives in their colourful costume as they moved from one well-stocked counter to another. Tinned goods of every description were available, and fresh milk and eggs at a reasonable price. Green vegetables and fresh fruit were expensive as might have been expected, and we decided that six shillings was too much to pay for one small cabbage.

From Karajok we journeyed on to Lakselv, past the 70th Parallel, and, at the head of Porsanger Fjord, we had our first glimpse of the Arctic Sea. I don't quite know what we were expecting, but any romantic notions that 'we were the first that ever burst into that silent sea' were rudely shattered by the roar of an aeroplane coming in to land on an airstrip by the sea.

We had coffee in the local hotel, and while we were there a thigh-booted, leather-jacketed figure stalked in. Henk, who could never resist the opportunity of making conversation with an interesting character, whatever his nationality, went over to speak to him.

'Hello,' said Henk breezily, 'Are you fishing?' 'No,' came the crisp reply, 'I'm flying.' For once Henk's instinct had let him down: his fisherman was the pilot of the plane. He returned to our table shaking with laughter. 'It was a bad identification,' he said, 'but he wasn't wearing his wings.'

We were soon on the road again heading almost due east through mile upon mile of remote upland country. We passed three farmsteads only in the next sixty miles. Eventually we halted in a valley where three levels of raised beach could clearly be seen in the glacial debris of gravels and boulders deposited there. Coltsfoot was almost in flower – we collected a few promising buds and they burst into bloom in the warmth of the car a few hours later when we resumed our journey. The first tiny mauve and yellow tundra flowers were showing on the mossy carpet. A few stunted birches were in tiny leaf and noticeably more advanced than those inland at Karigasniemi. Here on the coast we were to some extent under the Gulf Stream's kindly influence. Common Gulls were nesting along the shore, and an Eider Duck flew from a cranny between two boulders and disclosed its nest. Three huge grey-green eggs were lying there, but little eider down had as yet accumulated round them for warmth and protection.

Another spell of travel brought us to Adamsfjord where a mighty cataract came thundering down the mountain-side, dividing into greater and lesser falls – Adam and Eva – before plunging sheer into the Arctic Sea below. The day was now far advanced and we decided to halt for the night. We had supper and thought about having a reasonably early bedtime for a change.

Henk and Anneke were sensible and retired forthwith, but we decided otherwise. 'Mad dogs and Englishmen go out in the Midnight Sun,' muttered Tim as we set forth to climb the near-by hill. It seemed a pity to deny ourselves the pleasure of another photographic session. The sun, just clear of the horizon, had turned the cataract into molten gold. It would be difficult to capture such a sight, but it was worth trying.

What wildlife should we expect to find in a remote bay in the Arctic Sea? The following morning we decided to find out. But in an hour's walk we saw less than a score of birds. There were Arctic Ringed Plovers, Oyster-catchers, Hooded Crows, Velvet Scoters and a Rough-legged Buzzard, all of which we had seen before. One bird we had not met so far on our journey was there – a Ring Ouzel – a pleasant reminder of boyhood excursions in the Derbyshire hills.

So we continued our eastward journey. For the next three hours we traversed a world of upland snow-fields where drifts were still piled above car height on either side of the road. The surface was rough and loose, and we were a little apprehensive of what might lie ahead.

Half-way down one particularly impressive mountain we halted. On a steep fell-side on the other side of the valley reindeer were bunching together prior to crossing an upland snow-field where they would make a fine picture. While we were filming them one of the few cars we had seen on this remote stretch of road approached from the valley below. It halted and two Norwegian fishermen beckoned us to come and inspect their catch. They had fourteen fine salmon and they were ready for barter. We had a certain amount of language difficulty.

179

They could hardly speak a word of English and we were sadly deficient in Norwegian, but the word 'whisky' was common to both. However, we had to shake our heads. No whisky. How about coins? We produced a handful, and finally agreed on a sum that was the equivalent of twelve shillings – a fair price, we considered, for a sizeable salmon that would provide us with delicious salmon steaks for several meals to come.

Down now to the River Tana, considerably more impressive in size than when we had parted company with it two days before. We had an enjoyable run beside the river, then crossed a low-lying region of swamps and pools where Phalaropes reappeared, and where a pair of Curlews – officially out of their breeding-range – were nesting, and so we came to Varanger Fjord, our Ultima Thule. We drew off the road beside a gurgling stream. For the last few miles we had been aware of an increasing richness in the bird-life on the fjord shores. We had paused to watch twenty-five Red-breasted Mergansers swimming in a loose flock with Eider Ducks. A little further on we had seen ten Scoters swimming near the shore. Gulls and terns and waders were reappearing. The whole area had the right feel.

One thing was apparent, however – the drop in temperature. It was appreciably colder here in this extreme north-eastern tip of Lapland. A little further up the fjord and we should be looking across at Russia. Henk had been here before: he had warned us of 'Varanger Fjord weather'.

We finished our meal with a brew of hot cocoa and were grateful for its warmth. We distributed spare blankets and climbed into our sleeping-bags, but not before a hot water bottle had been dispatched to Anneke with the compliments of the management. It was accepted graciously but with reservations. In Varanger Fjord one should learn to be tough. One should not need these artificial aids.

A slight lift in the temperature the following morning made life decidedly more pleasant. We found we had drawn off the road close to a crumbling sand-cliff where newly-arrived Sand Martins were beginning to tunnel their holes. Hardly a trace remained of last year's excavations. The winter frost and the incessant winds had seen to that. The rate of weathering on a crumbling sand face such as this could be measured in feet rather than in inches every year.

We had a leisurely start to the day, and it was nearly noon when we arrived at the town of Vadso and back to civilization once more. A plume of smoke from the fish-fertilizer plant told us of the location of the town long before the houses came in sight. We found a news-paper kiosk and purchased a *Daily Telegraph* only five days old with all the latest cricket scores. We bought fresh milk and eggs, fruit, and chocolate, but all the time we were edging towards the eastern outskirts of the town, for in that direction lay our Vadso goal – the town rubbish dump. 'You simply must visit the Vadso rubbish dump,' we had been told by the Varanger Fjord en-thusiast we had met on Texel. 'There are Phalaropes and Stints and Shore-Larks, and you will be allowed about twenty minutes before you are asked to leave.' Henk confirmed this from personal experience on his previous trip. 'Twenty minutes if you're lucky. Fifteen minutes if not.' 'But why should we be moved on?' Henk

181

murmured something about 'installations'. It all sounded rather odd, but we pressed on.

Soon we came to the edge of the tipping area. It was the usual horrible, smelly mess of tins and garbage, of broken bicycles, discarded mattresses and other un-wanted domestic junk – a singularly unpromising place for an afternoon's bird-watching. Some children were sorting through the rubbish: one was proudly waving a broken parasol. True, there were two pairs of Shore-Larks picking their way through the debris, but the setting was hardly photogenic. And as for Phalaropes – where on earth in this murky region could they be found? We climbed a soil bank and looked over the other side. Before us lay a quite delightful little pool set in its own private marsh, the bounds of which were determined by a token fence – a single strand of wire that wasn't even of the familiar barbed variety. Five pairs of binoculars eagerly scanned the area: it was alive with birds. A dozen Phalaropes were swimming on the open water, and trotting along the edge of the pool were a dozen diminutive waders – hardly larger than sparrows – Temminck's and Little Stints.

Just beyond the marsh and within the wired area was a curious metal tower festooned with hardwear of one sort and other – clearly an 'installation'. But we had eyes only for the birds. In a fever of impatience we scrambled over the strand of wire and surged across the marsh to the edge of the pool. The Phalaropes scarcely moved: some of the Stints flipped across to the other side: others merely trotted away along the muddy edge for a few yards and resumed feeding. Tripods were spreadeagled and their legs thrust into the marshy ground. Cameras with sinister, looming telephoto lenses swung into action. Five fervent photographers, completely absorbed in their craft, went prowling round the pool. But it was too good to last: Nemesis was about to overtake us. Not until he was twenty yards away did any of us notice the oncoming Arm of the Law. What made him doubly impressive was the uniform he wore. We were being confronted not by the civil police: we were face to face with the Norwegian Army.

'You are not allowed here. Photography is forbidden.' The voice was polite but curt. We were addressed in our own language, spoken with a decidedly American accent. We explained about the birds. 'You will find them all in a lake in the hills behind the town. You cannot stay here. This is Top Secret.'

We made our apologies and departed. When we were out of sight, Henk consulted his watch. He shook his head. 'They are tightening up,' he said. 'Fourteen minutes dead. Too bad!'

14

Varanger Fjord and its Birds

FROM Vadso the road along Varanger Fjord followed
the shore-line closely. Away in the distance beyond
the coastal hills we could see, across the grey-green
water, the grim, snow-streaked mountains of Russia.
The further we progressed along the fjord the more
birds we began to see. Three pairs of Goosanders made
a memorable sight as they swam close inshore. Eider
ducks and drakes were in every inlet. Wherever there
was a patch of marshy ground Ruffs showed up in belligerent groups, and on drier ground the first Turnstones
began to appear. Henk said that these were only isolated
pairs for we were not yet in the real breeding-area.
Ahead of us we could see a small fishing village which
the map told us was Saltjern. A hundred yards from the
village we passed through a succession of little stone-
walled meadows on either side of the road, many of
them not much larger than tennis courts. The noise of
our passage sent scores of Arctic Terns up into the air.
They screeched in protest, and then, when we slowed
down and came to a halt, they descended and alighted on
their nests some of which were only four or five yards
from the road. I was tempted to get out of the car
because two Turnstones were seen to be running about

amongst the terns. But Henk counselled patience. We should find all the Turnstones we wanted a few miles further on. And so we passed through Saltjern, a strangely silent and deserted-looking hamlet, and were just leaving the last of the houses when we came into a little bay where scores of Eiders were floating on the tide or resting on the weed-strewn rocks. Immediately we noticed a strangeness about one large and compact group of them. These birds were much smaller than normal Eiders, and they had a different plumage-pattern. We halted the car, clapped binoculars to our eyes, and stared incredulously. These were Steller's Eiders, one of the true European rarities, and they were less than fifty yards away. Ten were handsome drakes and forty-two were brown ducks or immature non-breeding birds. When the drakes stood upright on the rocks, dark red patches like rust stains showed on their underparts. It was low tide, and presently, while watching the Steller's Eiders, we became aware of movements in the seaweed near at hand. Inconspicuously feeding almost at our feet were Dunlins, Purple Sandpipers and Stints. There was no need for us to go any further. By the side of the road was a dusty, level platform that would take a caravan. What better than to draw off here, and have the pleasure – surely unique – of feasting on salmon steaks while gazing out from the caravan windows at a flock of Steller's Eiders swimming in the bay. There may be a hotel somewhere in the world that could afford a comparable service, but I very much doubt it.

After breakfast the following day we decided to spend the morning exploring our immediate surroundings. A low cliff with attractive rock terraces fronted the fjord at this point, and here we found the nests of Herring Gulls, and an isolated pair of Arctic Terns that mobbed us repeatedly when we stood over their nest. Across the road, a mere fifty yards away, a pair of Arctic Ringed Plovers were nesting in the tundra vegetation, and – best of all – in a little grass meadow a stone's throw from the caravan, Henk found the nest of a Temminck's Stint, no bigger than a Skylark's, and containing as yet but three diminutive but beautifully-marked eggs. A new pipit soon came to our notice. This bird would rise with rapidly whirring wings in a sudden, steep ascent, and then, having reached its zenith, would float back to earth in a vertical fall with wings half-spread and tail fanned out – the nearest thing to a parachute that a bird could possibly achieve. This was the arctic-breeding Red-throated Pipit. We searched for its nest in vain, but found two Meadow Pipits' while doing so, and a Redshank's with a full clutch.

After lunch we decided to leave the caravan and explore by car the fjord shores towards Vardo. At Ekkero a great cliff of bedded shale jutted out into the fjord. Even at a distance the clamour of nesting sea-birds reached our ears, but when we finally reached the cliff edge and looked down on the crowded ledges, the sight and sound – and smell – of countless thousands of Kittiwake Gulls was well-nigh overpowering. A narrow path threaded its way along the cliffs midway between sea and sky. It required a steady nerve and a good head for heights to tackle it. It was a cliff path used by generations of fisherfolk at Ekkero for the harvesting of Kittiwakes' eggs, but the number of nests within reach of the egg-collectors was infinitesimal. A few pairs of Razorbills and Guillemots were seen, and some twenty pairs of Black Guillemots were nesting in rock crevices in the lower levels of the cliff. Sufficient boulders were dislodged in one place for a view of the two eggs to be obtained. In the auk world it seems strange that the Black Guillemot which lays two eggs should be so much rarer than the normal Guillemot which lays but one.

With our ears full of sea-bird sound we retraced our steps to the car and proceeded along a very rough-surfaced road in the direction of Vardo. On either side of the road we were now looking out on typical tundra country, with occasional pools and stony ridges to break the monotony. Suddenly Henk gave a shout. 'Turnstones are breeding here!' About thirty yards from the road a small blob of white showed above the prevailing duns and browns of the tundra vegetation. The car came to a sudden stop, and immediately a Turnstone sprang from its place of concealment and flew off chittering harshly. We tumbled out of the car and ran across the intervening space. There, in a slight depression, lay four dark, greenish-brown eggs, very densely mottled and wonderfully inconspicuous as they lay in the nesting-hollow open to the sky. Another ambition achieved!

In the next half-mile and in a quarter of an hour's travel we found five more nests, all containing four eggs, through watching out for that tell-tale blob of white on the head of the sitting bird. And the Turnstone's chief predator was there, too. Two pairs of Arctic Skuas were lording it over this Turnstone territory. They were the robber barons, and formidable ones, too, when we trespassed on their domain. These great, dark pirate gulls came swooping down from behind, more than ready to deliver a stinging buffet on the back of the head of anyone caught unawares. Henk advised us to carry a stick with a handkerchief tied to the top. This had the desired effect of keeping these menacing birds at bay.

One interesting thing we noted about the behaviour of Turnstones in this open country was the way in which they approached their nests. Most waders make a hesitant, zig-zag approach on foot. It was not so with the Turnstones. Again and again we watched a bird that we had flushed return to its nest. The approach was always the same, providing we were sufficiently far away and allowing it to behave normally. From a distance of perhaps a hundred yards a bird would suddenly take to the air and head straight for the nesting-area, flying Partridge-like a few feet from the ground. When immediately over the eggs it would drop like a stone, and in an instant be lost to view – except, perhaps, for the little white blob on its head, but even this would hardly show when the vegetation was a little higher. The Turnstone seems to have a built-in awareness of its own highly-coloured, boldly-chequered plumage pattern. If it followed the normal mode of wader nest-approach – the cautious zig-zagging to and fro – it would be in danger of betraying the whereabouts of its nest every time it returned home. Instead, it has perfected a direct, flying approach which culminates in a vanishing trick. It is very well done.

By now we were beginning to realize how quickly time had slipped away, and how appallingly hungry we were. We had had a sandwich lunch at midday, but it was now half-past eight in the evening. Not only did we feel desperately hollow, but with the sun now low in the sky a deadly chill was creeping over this arctic world. We huddled in the car and shivered, and hurried home. It required a sustained burst of calor gas to warm up the caravan on our arrival there. We awoke to grey skies after a chilly night, and we could sense a threat of snow from the north which materialized in occasional light showers that persisted for the rest of the day. Fore-warned we all wore double thicknesses of clothing. It seemed absurd in mid-June to be putting on two pairs of trousers, two sweaters and an anorak, but it was a wise precaution and we all felt better that day for the additional clothing we had on.

After breakfast I had half an hour in a hide of heaped boulders by the water's edge. A mixed flock of Common and Steller's Eiders came swimming in with the tide. They clambered on to a hummock of seaweed-covered rock, and I had the satisfaction of filming them there. Afterwards we set out for the Turnstone territory on a second visit. We dearly wanted to try for photographs but the light deteriorated as we travelled along. It was impossibly dull when we reached the tundra terrain where they were breeding so we decided to press on. A few miles along the road we investigated an area of pool and marsh but it was unproductive. With the light now rapidly improving we decided to return. As we reached the Turnstone area the sun broke through and an hour's good photographic light seemed assured. We made for the first nest that we had found the day before. It was nearest to the road and the birds should be used to the

189

sight and sound of passing cars. As we edged the car off the road and slowly bumped our way towards the nest the handsome male bird who was sitting on the eggs suddenly flew away chittering explosively. We stopped and kept quite still. In a few moments he returned and dropped from the air on to the nest. The car nosed forward another yard or two. Away he went a second time, but again returned as soon as the car stood still. And so, little by little, we approached to within ten yards of the nest. First photographs were taken, and another approach was made – eight yards, then six yards, then four yards. There were five of us in the car, but in spite of a veritable battery of lenses aiming at him the Turnstone would not be deterred. When we were only four yards away he did a couple of running approaches, and he swore at us a good deal for the inconvenience we were causing him. But in the end he was so emboldened by familiarity with this great looming vehicle and the silent, slow-moving figures within that it became necessary for one of us to wave a handkerchief from the back of the car to persuade him to leave the eggs. We filmed and photographed him from near and far, at rest and in motion – flying, running, walking, standing, sitting. 'Total photographic cover,' I said to Henk at last. 'No, no,' he said. 'You forget the aerial shot . . . a hole in the floor of the car . . . and we drive right over him!' Hardly a serious suggestion, but it showed how fantastically tame the Turnstone had now become. And all the time the sun was shining, and those black and white and chestnut-chequered markings stood boldly out against the darker, tundra background – a very handsome and distinguished-looking bird. I cannot recall a more exhilarating hour in thirty years of bird photography. Moreover, this delightful encounter had strengthened an already strong personal regard that I have always had for this particular bird. A close companion on many a vigil on the tide-line, the Turnstone was an old and honoured friend. A bird that shows decidedly individual character, as he does, stands out from the rest. He seems to know what he wants to do in this life, and he doesn't believe in doing things by halves.

In excellent spirits we trundled back to the road again and went on towards Vardo in search of other promising haunts. A few miles on and we were surprised to find a familiar car drawn up by the roadside. It was Ralph and John again, all the way from Karigasniemi. They, too, had felt the call of Varanger Fjord, and here they were exploring an area of pool and marsh that lay between the road and the sea. They had already discovered nests of Willow Grouse and Lapland Bunting. To these we shortly added Black-throated Diver, Arctic Tern, Phalarope and Dunlin. It was an area of fresh water, bogland and heath that held, within a few acres, a wonderfully rich fauna. We decided that this should be the scene of our photographic operations on the morrow. We would erect hides and then go into Vardo, and have a photographic session on our return.

However, on the following day it did not quite work out as intended. We erected a hide at the Lapland Bunting's nest and did some preliminary trimming of a willow that overlooked the diver's nest. We then proceeded to Vardo, a busy fishing town on an offshore island and accessible only by a ferry that went at hourly intervals. A keen wind chilled us while we waited, and the crossing though short was distinctly rough. By the time we reached the town our main concern was to find somewhere for warmth and shelter from the wind. We discovered just the right place – a coffee bar with central heating. After half an hour of thawing out while we sipped hot coffee we were ready to visit the local shops and buy much-needed stores. In a rather desultory fashion we wandered from shop to shop, and gradually and quite unintentionally we separated. Henk and Anneke had already disappeared, having urgent business to conduct in a local bank. But time was getting on and the next ferry was due to leave shortly, so four out of five of our party reassembled at the embarkation point. But my brother was missing. Time meant very little to him. He had last been seen inquiring the price of colour film in a chemist's shop. What should we do? The ferry was due to sail. It was bitterly cold waiting there on the quayside. Across the water was the car: at least we could sit inside and be out of the wind. So we crossed over, and huddled in the car for an hour in growing exasperation. When at last he arrived on the next ferry, an hour later, my brother's temper was as frayed as ours. 'A properly disorganized affair!' he snorted. 'What do you mean by going off like that?' I think we were all too flabbergasted to reply, but I know that we were perilously near to a first-class family row. It was only the presence of Anneke and Henk that saved the day. The perilous moment passed. The Englishmen put on their stiff upper lip, and the party set off for home. The hours had slipped by. It was too late now to attempt any photography. From that standpoint it was a wasted day – but it proved not to be entirely profitless in other ways. On the way

Dunlin approaching nest.
Varanger Fjord.

11

Male Turnstone nesting on the open
tundra on the fjord shores.

Arctic Skua on defensive patrol
in its breeding territory.
Varanger Fjord.

12

Redwing feeding half-grown young.
Karigasniemi.   Finnish Lapland.

home we saw, floating out at sea, a large flotilla of
Eiders – about a hundred and fifty birds in all. We halted
to check for Steller's Eiders, but found to our delight not
Steller's but King Eiders swimming there. There were
six males and a score of females and juveniles. The
orange shields on the heads of the males, their grey
heads, black backs, and the white rounded spots near
their tails were completely diagnostic. This was an
entirely new species for us all. We returned home
greatly cheered by the sight – and it was salmon for
supper again. Henk had purchased another fine fish for
ten shillings.

During the evening the wind dropped and the temperature rose appreciably. A warm front was passing
over, and gentle rain began to fall and continued to do so
all night long. A dull morning succeeded a wet night,
and we confined our activities to an exploration of the
boggy heathland immediately behind our base. Phalaropes were on all the little pools. Vigilant Turnstones
stood guard over nesting territories on higher ground.
Bar-tailed Godwits and Northern Golden Plovers were
breeding in the area. Lapland Buntings, attractive little
birds with rufous nape patches, were abundant and four
nests were found. And high in the air, once more, the
Lapland horseman went cantering past – we were in
Jack Snipe country again. It began to rain heavily as we
were returning to the caravan, so we retired to our
bunks and had a long, long sleep. It rained for twelve
hours and for twelve hours we slept solidly, making
good the deficiencies of the past few weeks. Greatly
refreshed we rose the following morning to find the rain
abating and the sun struggling to break through. We

decided to have a photographic day in the lake and marsh area where we had found so many good nests. We had an interesting multiple photographic session, beginning with a successful stalk of the Willow Grouse sitting on her darkly-mottled eggs. We then photographed and filmed with varying success a Dunlin, a Lapland Bunting and a Black-throated Diver. Three more Dunlins' nests were found, and, just as we were leaving for home, a Red-necked Phalarope's. If we had had more time we might also have tracked down Purple Sandpiper and Little Stint, for both were seen behaving in a suspicious manner.

On the return journey we were fortunate to find the Steller's Eider flock feeding in deep water quite close to a cliffy shore. They were all there one moment swimming on the surface: the next and they had dived out of sight. Twenty seconds later up they would come, shooting out of the water as though jet-propelled. Then, after a short pause, down they would dive again. The complete unanimity in this flock of over fifty birds was remarkable. They appeared and disappeared *in toto*. They might have been executing a military exercise. When they performed the disappearing trick we ran forwards towards them: the moment they surfaced we froze. In this way, in five or six forward rushes, we covered the hundred yards from the road to the cliff edge, and now had them within good photographic range. Before long they tired of feeding and came swimming ashore. It was a very pleasing conclusion to our Varanger Fjord adventure, and the fifty feet of film that I expended on the Steller's Eiders on that final afternoon were some of the best of the trip.

As the light was still very good – strong, low sunlight with plenty of contrast in the shadows – we visited the Arctic Terns at the entrance to Saltjern village, and obtained photographs and ciné shots from the windows of the car of these graceful and obliging birds.

There was one bird that we had left to the end – the Temminck's Stint in the little hay meadow less than fifty yards from the caravan. We wanted to make sure that she was sitting securely on a full clutch of eggs before attempting photography. We were due to depart from Saltjern to start the homeward trail the following afternoon. That gave us a full morning which should be all the time that we would need. It ought to be quite easy to go through the necessary preliminaries of moving a hide gradually nearer in the time available. At five a.m. the sun was shining brilliantly, but by six o'clock when we proposed making a start the sun withdrew behind an ominous bank of cloud, and half an hour later a steady rain began. In between the showers we erected a hide – at first twenty yards away, and then, when accepted, at ten. But it was now mid-morning and the rain was tippling down. We could not operate in these conditions, and decided to wait for a clearance. But it never came. By mid-afternoon we had to admit defeat. The hide was taken down: the caravan hitched to the Bedford – and we were off.

We were hoping to take the alternative route back to Ivalo through Utsjoki and across the Tana ferry, but there was a possibility that the ferry might not be open yet because of flood conditions in the late spring season. By taking this route we should have avoided the stretch of a hundred and fifty miles across the high Norwegian fells, where narrow mountain roads could be very awkward for a car with caravan in tow if a heavy lorry coming in the opposite direction were to be encountered. It was for this reason that we had already decided on an all-night journey – and on a Sunday night, too – to cut down the risk to a minimum. As we feared, the Utsjoki ferry was still not open, so we set our faces grimly to the mountain route. A steady rain accompanied us all the way up the Tana valley, but as we began to climb up into the high fell country the rain turned to sleet and then to snow.

For hour upon hour we trundled on at a steady thirty-five miles an hour. Weariness overtook us one by one. By midnight – a pale white midnight in this snowy wilderness – the three in the rear seat were fast asleep. By 1 a.m., I, who sat by the driver to give him moral support, had also succumbed. Grimly, relentlessly, my brother drove on. Only when Borselv had been passed and the back of the journey well and truly broken did he halt. It was 2.30 a.m. Waking from our uneasy sleep in cold and cramped attitudes, we staggered towards our sleeping berths. Life was at a very low ebb: we were even too tired to brew up a hot drink.

But it is surprising how a few hours of sleep can restore morale. We were up betimes in brightening weather, and soon reached Lakselv on Porsanger Fjord, and from there journeyed due south to Karajok where we filmed sundry Lap characters in costume – and so back to Karigasniemi and our caravan site on the roadside gravels. Our snowdrift had almost melted. The birch trees were bursting into leaf: the countryside was transformed. We paid a final visit to Mount Aligas. The

Bar-tailed Godwit and the Whimbrel had both hatched their eggs and the young had dispersed. The Golden Plover was still sitting hard on four eggs, but the elusive Dotterels were not seen. Everywhere, both on the mountain and back in camp, there was a feeling that the breeding-season was now far advanced. Bird song had quietened down. Bluethroats were almost silent; Redwings far less vocal, and even the Brambling's wheezy notes were now but seldom heard.

We spent the following morning taking satisfactory final shots of a Redwing feeding half-grown young. In the late afternoon we said farewell to Henk and Anneke. They were now installed in their little 'dog-house' – Henk often referred to the Lap houses in this affectionate way. This miniature Youth Hostel of theirs had its own stove, its reindeer skins for bedding, its axe and saw. They had about them all the necessities for the simple life, and they had another six weeks in which to enjoy their beloved Lapland. We parted rather wistfully: our Lapland days were numbered.

And so began the long trek home. We left Karigas-niemi in the early evening and headed south, past Lake Inari where, towards midnight, on a pine-covered hillside, we saw an elk in noble silhouette against the skyline. We drew off the road shortly afterwards and had a meal before turning in for a few hours' sleep. For the first time since coming to Lapland we found the mosquitoes troublesome, and we realized how extraordinarily fortunate we had been to visit Lapland for the first time in a late spring. After a few hours' rest we were on the road again, travelling under grey skies along gravelled roads now greatly improved because the

road-scrapers were at work smoothing out the corrugated surfaces. Between Ivalo and Sodankyla rain set in
and continued hour upon hour for the rest of the day.
Near Petulka we came upon two rain-sodden travellers
foot-slogging down the highway heading south. They
looked as though they would welcome a lift and so we
stopped, and they clambered into the car. Fido was a
Dane and Eddie an Italian. They had met in Paris a year
before, and planned a trip to Lapland. Fido could not
speak Italian: Eddie could not speak Danish. For three
months they had travelled together conversing in broken
English. Their possessions were lumped on their backs –
a few clothes, cooking utensils and some food. They had
sketch-books, an assortment of pipes, and plenty of
tobacco. They had a couple of blankets each, and two
sheets of stout polythene – one to act as a ground-sheet,
the other as a shelter above. They were on a working
holiday, having hitch-hiked through Norway to Trond-
heim, and there been taken on as deck-hands on a tramp
steamer working its way from port to port round the
North Cape to Kirkenes. From there they had struck
across country by map and compass towards Lake Inari.
They had run into weather trouble, been taken on as
farm-hands on a remote Lap farm for a few days while
they dried off, and were now heading for Kiruna, 'the
Iron Mountain', hoping for jobs in the mines to put them
in funds again.

We spent the night at Rovaniemi on the municipal site
by the riverside, where a score of tents and caravans of a
dozen different nationalities were now installed. Fido
and Eddie slept in the Bedford in borrowed blankets
while their own had a chance to dry off. We paid a brief

visit to the Rovaniemi marsh on the outskirts of the town. Three weeks ago the vegetation of the marshland was brown and lifeless, and the distant hills white with snow. Now the hills were green and the marsh was white – white with a million tufts of cotton-grass in flower. Lush green vegetation was springing up in the meadows, and, instead of buttercups, globe-flowers spread a cloth of gold over the Lapland fields. We recollected the gold of dandelions on the roadsides of Denmark; the gold of kingcups on Swedish lakeside shores, and the gold of lichen on the rocks of Varanger Fjord: and now this final gift of Lapland gold – the glow of globe-flowers by the Rovaniemi road. A few other flowers were coming into early bloom – campions were flaunting their red rosettes in wayside ditches, and a very pale cranesbill, seemingly drained of all its colour by the winter darkness and cold, was bravely exposing its first fragile blooms.

In the herbage by the highway that ran through the marsh, and a few yards only from the traffic now constantly streaming past, we found our last Lapland nest – a Temminck's Stint's with a full clutch of eggs. If time had allowed and traffic been less persistent we could have photographed that little wader there and then, but it was hardly fair to erect a hide by the roadside and so attract attention to the nest.

So we journeyed on and into southern Lapland, overtaking spring with every mile we travelled. The day was warm and the countryside fresh and green. We had a lunch-stop beside a copse in which Siskins were singing. To give stability to the caravan while we lunched inside, the back legs were wound down. Afterwards we explored the little copse and found a wild azalea with creamy-white flowers, and the pink bells of whinberries nodding in the breeze. The sun was warm on our backs. We had lunched well, and no doubt we were more fatigued than we realized by the endless judder of tyres bouncing on the corrugated surface of the Lapland roads. We were certainly feeling relaxed – a little too relaxed: we were off our guard. It was time we were moving. While the others piled into the car I went through the routine check of seeing that the caravan door was locked and the gear stowed, but I failed – I failed utterly and miserably – to make one other necessary check. I jumped in beside the driver and off we went – for ten grinding yards. An appalling sound of scraping metal accompanied our abortive start. We stopped, jumped out, and ran to the rear to inspect the damage. We had committed the caravanner's unforgivable sin – we had started off without winding up the back legs. They were now horribly bent and twisted backwards, and of course totally unserviceable. It was indeed a grim discovery. Somehow we must force them back into a position where they would not scrape the ground, and we must lash them with ropes to the main chassis. It was an arduous task. Greatly sobered, we proceeded on our way. My brother said very little. He drove grimly forward, but his chin jutted out defiantly, and the expression on his face was Churchillian. His legs may have been smitten off but he could still fight on his stumps. We were nearly two thousand miles from home, but, legs or no legs, we would make it. And we did.

We spent the night at Haparanda where, three weeks earlier, we had first felt the shock of the arctic cold. Now the air was balmy and heavy with the scent of new-mown grass. We backed the caravan down a shelving sandy beach and into the river, and we hurled bucketfuls of water at it to remove layer upon layer of encrusted mud from the Lapland roads. In a surprisingly short time it was fresh and clean-gleaming once more. We tried not to notice the hideous deformity of its mangled legs. Eddie and Fido paid us the compliment of making, from their own stores, a brew of English tea of a richness unsurpassed. We went into town and bought souvenirs. The youth of Haparanda was out for its evening stroll. Girls were wandering about in sweaters embroidered with vaguely-familiar, half-remembered names like 'Stones' and 'Beatles', and back at the camp-site transistors were softly playing folk music from Radio Helsinki. I paused to listen, and as I did so the music changed, and the haunting notes of a girl singing 'Greensleeves' came floating out on the evening air. The words were Finnish, but all England was in that song. I was suddenly filled with an intense longing for home. It was time I returned to my own patient Greensleeves. My ambition had been fulfilled. I had been North with the Spring, and nothing could ever alter that: but the sooner I returned now the happier I should be.

We dropped Fido and Eddie at Tore early the following morning, and pressed on south down the E.4. We took turns at the wheel and went on relentlessly, hardly stopping at all for the next twenty-six hours. We virtually covered seven hundred miles non-stop. It was a hard day's night. We strode in seven-league boots from April apple-blossom in northern Sweden to June roses in the Stockholm suburbs. We drove all through the

Swedish 'Midsommer Night', while festive parties were taking place up and down the length and breadth of the land. Cars were garlanded with greenery, and poles, festooned with leafy boughs, stood on the crowded village greens.

The following day we reached Halsingborg and crossed over to Denmark, to Helsingor where we visited the castle of Hamlet fame at nearby Elsinore. At the maritime museum there the custodian, noting my month-old beard, now entering its distinguished phase, addressed me deferentially as 'Captain'. We inquired despairingly about the possibility of a crossing from Esbjerg to Harwich. We were convinced that such an inquiry was really a waste of time, and were all prepared for the long haul down to Calais, but, to our delight were told that we could have a reservation the following day for car and caravan and three passengers. There was only one snag. It meant travelling First Class. A hasty calculation showed that our Sterling reserves would just about meet the additional expense, so we took the plunge. The following afternoon three remarkably scruffy-looking Englishmen who had been roughing it in the wilds for the last two months – and looked it – went on board the spotlessly clean vessel that was to deliver them to Harwich and their homeland the following morning. Instead of disappearing down a ladder and into the stokehold where, from their appearance, they properly belonged, the three scruffy ones proceeded with as much dignity as they could muster up the stairway to the First Class deck, to cabins where bowls of fruit awaited them, and hot baths, and carpets underfoot, and soft upholstered chairs. It was a perfect end to our adventure. Wearied by travel but filled with a great contentment we lay stretched out in luxurious ease on the sun-deck. Our journey was over: we could afford to relax.

Apart from having had a wonderful holiday what had we achieved? Over forty species of birds that were new to us had been sighted during our nine thousand miles of travel. We had found the nests and eggs of no less than eighteen wader species. But it had been more than a fascinating pursuit of rare and interesting birds. We had been privileged to visit some of the loveliest wildlife areas still left in Europe. We had met fellow enthusiasts and shared their company and their hopes and plans for conservation projects in the future. At the start of the journey we had passed through countries where the pressures exerted by man on the creatures that share the countryside with him are already great, and will continue to increase. We had finished our journey in the unspoilt, incredibly beautiful wilderness that fronts the Arctic Sea – a wilderness in which man has, as yet, scarcely left his mark.

For many species of birds this is still a vast, undisturbed breeding-area where, in comparative safety, they may rear their young. For ducks and geese and waders it is the great reservoir of European bird-life, from which migrating streams pour south each year when the brief arctic summer comes to its sudden close. Surely the prosperous countries of Western Europe through which they must pass on their journeyings – surely they can afford a few acres of marshland here – an area of mud-flats and undrained fenland there – a chain of little oases where some at least may pass through in safety. Surely,

too, in the last twenty years, enough evidence has accumulated on the deadly effects of toxic chemicals indis-
criminately scattered on the land to stir the conscience
of civilized man and cause him to think again – to recon-
sider the whole question of his stewardship of the good
earth.

I should like to think that my grandchildren and great-
grandchildren, on a similar journey, will still see Little
Egrets and Flamingoes on the étangs of the Camargue,
and Avocets and Greylag Geese in a Belgian reserve. I
hope that there will still be Ruffs and Godwits and
Spoonbills in the Dutch polders, and Black Terns and
Harriers and Little Gulls in the reedy meres of northern
Denmark. I hope that Cranes can still be seen from a
watchtower in a Swedish marsh, and that Bluethroats
will be singing in the Lapland birches, and Phalaropes
spinning on an arctic pool. Without them the landscape
would be immeasurably the poorer, and the journey
almost pointless. If we denude the countryside of its
wildlife – its mammals and birds, its insects and flowers
– what we have left would be incomparably dull. It is a
frightening thought that Man, today, holds the wildlife
of the world in the hollow of his hand – a thoughtless
squeeze and much of it can be extinguished for ever.
These lovely creatures are so vulnerable, and we are
losing them so fast. If only people really cared . . . ! A
change in our basic attitudes to the beautiful, the wild
and the rare is desperately needed. For the sake of
generations yet unborn I only hope that this change will
have come in time.

Index

205